Asperger Syndrome in the Inclusive Classroom

Asperger Syndrome
in the Inclusive Classroom
Advice and Strategies for Teachers

Stacey W. Betts, Dion E. Betts,
and Lisa N. Gerber-Eckard

Foreword by Peter Riffle

Jessica Kingsley Publishers
London and Philadelphia

First published in 2007
by Jessica Kingsley Publishers
116 Pentonville Road
London N1 9JB, UK
and
400 Market Street, Suite 400
Philadelphia, PA 19106, USA

www.jkp.com

Library of Congress Cataloging in Publication Data
Betts, Stacey W. (Stacey Waldman), 1964-
  Asperger syndrome in the inclusive classroom : advice and strategies for teachers / Stacey W. Betts, Dion
E. Betts and Lisa N. Gerber-Eckard ; foreword by Peter Riffle.
    p. cm.
  Includes bibliographical references and index.
  ISBN-13: 978-1-84310-840-5 (pbk.)
  1. Autistic children--Education. 2. Asperger's syndrome. 3. Inclusive education. I. Betts, Dion E. (Dion
Emile), 1963- II. Gerber-Eckard, Lisa N., 1967- III. Title.
  LC4717.B48 2007
  371.94--dc22

                                                            2006036801

British Library Cataloguing in Publication Data
A CIP catalogue record for this book is available from the British Library

ISBN 978 1 84310 840 5

Printed and bound in the United States by
Thomson-Shore, Inc.

I wish to dedicate my contribution to this book to my five children, Joshua, Jacob, Daniel, Dora, and Sarah. You surprise me every day with your insight, intelligence, and humor. I love you.

I also want to thank my parents for always telling me that it is important to try hard in school and that doing well in school is a great achievement. You were right.

Finally, I am grateful to my husband Dion for working so hard, which allows me to stay home with the children, write books, and practice yoga. Thanks, Dion. I appreciate all your hard work and support.

Stacey W. Betts

I wish to thank the courageous and thoughtful teachers who discovered that working with students with Asperger Syndrome can be challenging and interesting. Their spirit of care, goodwill, and willingness to learn about students with this disorder is enlightening and heartening.

I could not be more fortunate than to spend my life with Stacey, who is a wonderful partner and wife. She is intelligent, warm, and supportive of my professional and personal goals.

Dion E. Betts

My contribution to this book is dedicated to my family whose love and patience allowed me to share these important stories and methods of teaching the student with Asperger Syndrome.

It is also dedicated to all those who read and implement strategies in this book. We all make a difference, each in our own way. May each of you continue to make a difference in the lives of those you touch.

Lisa N. Gerber-Eckard

Acknowledgments

We would like to acknowledge all of the teachers who have worked with our son Joshua over the years, especially Miss Michelle Mohn and Mrs. Shari Brabant. Although these teachers never take credit for Joshua's success, we know that they had a direct impact on his academic and social development in school. We also want to thank Mrs. Christine Smolar for helping Joshua with his daily organizational and social challenges. Your warmth and patience helped Joshua navigate the stresses of sixth grade.

Stacey W. Betts and Dion E. Betts

I would like to acknowledge the outstanding teachers of South Western School District who share their enthusiasm, talent, and love of children every day in the classroom. Your students, their families, and others who read this book appreciate your time and effort. May your passion continue throughout your teaching career.

Lisa N. Gerber-Eckard

Contents

A Note on the Book

The authors suggest that parents and school personnel have a professional experienced in the field of Pervasive Developmental Disorders conduct educational testing on a student if school personnel believe the student to have Asperger Syndrome. Testing can help determine other difficulties that may have an educational impact on the student. Such additional information can help school teams devise and implement appropriate educational programming suitable for the individual student.

Additionally, some students with Asperger Syndrome may have other medical diagnoses. Parents should consult a physician regarding their child's specific diagnosis before acting upon some of the recommendations made in this book.

The stories and strategies presented in this book are a compilation of the authors' and teachers' experiences regarding teaching students with Asperger Syndrome. Therefore, any likeness to actual individuals is purely coincidental and unintended.

Disclaimer

For the sake of clarity in the text, unless clearly stated otherwise, the pronoun "he" is used throughout for a student with Asperger Syndrome and "she" is used to refer to a teacher.

Foreword

"You're getting a child with Asperger Syndrome!"

"What? Is it contagious? By the way, what is it?"

The preceding conversation probably takes place frequently across the country as a new school year approaches. The majority of teachers, along with most of the population, do not have a clue what a child with Asperger Syndrome acts like. Added to that problem is that teachers will most likely assume a correlation between the child's idiosyncrasies and low mental ability. This assumption, along with many other misguided thoughts about Asperger Syndrome, is not true. *Asperger Syndrome in the Inclusive Classroom: Advice and Strategies for Teachers* will become a "security blanket" for teachers first experiencing Asperger Syndrome in their classroom.

Before a teacher can successfully teach a child with Asperger Syndrome, she must understand the complicated and unique characteristics that accompany this syndrome. It is critically important that teachers approach having a child with Asperger Syndrome in the classroom as a learning situation for everyone involved. All of us are different from each other in many ways, just as we are similar in others. Students will pick up verbal and non-verbal clues from the teacher about whether or not to accept the new kid who "acts differently than we do."

This book is unparalleled in its approach to working with these youngsters. Stacey and Dion Betts have a personal interest in this syndrome since one of their own children has Asperger Syndrome. They know first-hand what it is like to raise a child with this disorder. In order to write this book, Stacey and Dion Betts and Lisa Gerber-Eckard have talked with scores of parents and veteran teachers who have developed techniques to work successfully with these children. Lisa has also taught children with Asperger Syndrome.

This text deals with the many different situations that arise when a student with Asperger Syndrome enters a new school setting. Change is frequently unsettling for many children, but for students with Asperger Syndrome it is even more so. The book discusses adaptations in the classroom, teaching of academic subjects, special subject classes, unstructured school time, and social and emotional concerns of children with Asperger Syndrome. *Asperger Syndrome in the Inclusive Classroom: Advice and Strategies for Teachers* is a common-sense approach to working with these children.

Teachers who read this book will now say, "I'm getting a child with Asperger Syndrome; let's work together and make this a positive experience for everyone."

Peter Riffle
2005 National Veterans of Foreign Wars Citizenship
and Education Teacher of the Year;
2000 Disney American Teacher Award Special Education Honoree

Introduction

Children who have Asperger Syndrome manifest symptoms of this disorder in various ways. Prior to attending school, parents often learn about their child's diagnosis and use different strategies to help them cope with difficulties that the child may face throughout the day.

However, when these children reach school age, they spend the majority of their day outside the home, in a school environment. This change of setting can cause anxiety for most children. For a child with Asperger Syndrome, the school setting can often be shocking and disorienting.

Students with Asperger Syndrome need special accommodations made to their school day to make the environment more comfortable and safe for them. These students do not absorb the rules of the school easily or quickly. They need support throughout the day from school staff so that they can function and learn at school.

Much of the difference between a student with Asperger Syndrome and a "typical" student is the way in which students with Asperger Syndrome interpret the environment and their world. Many individuals find students with Asperger Syndrome to be "quirky" or "weird" due to the students' behaviors. Students with Asperger Syndrome often show their stress overtly – for example, by flapping their arms, talking to themselves, losing control, or crying.

Additionally, students with Asperger Syndrome can respond to school events in non-typical ways. For example, moving from class to class can be difficult for these students, and can lead to them losing their way or becoming upset during these transition times. Other events such as assemblies can easily cause sensory overload for students with

Asperger Syndrome. Many school activities that may not bother the majority of students become major stressors for students with Asperger Syndrome.

The number of students with Autism Spectrum Disorders, including those with Asperger Syndrome, has risen drastically over the past 20 years. Both experienced and new teachers need more information to teach students with Asperger Syndrome. More students are entering school with this disorder. Unfortunately, the first exposure that many teachers have to Asperger Syndrome occurs on the first day of school when the student with this disorder enters the classroom.

This book is based on the experiences of teachers who have successfully taught students with Asperger Syndrome. These teachers discovered that instead of feeling anxiety about having students with this disorder in their classroom, they began to appreciate the challenges and rewards of teaching these students. When they have adequate information and ideas, teachers can become innovative and imaginative in their accommodations and techniques to help these students navigate their school day. Often, teachers can make minor changes in the environment and instruction and see successful results for students with Asperger Syndrome.

As an example, one teacher had positive results using a simple idea to help a student go from class to class with minimal problems. As mentioned above, students with Asperger Syndrome often have difficulty with transition periods, such as when the students change classrooms. This teacher uses a "pass the baton" approach in which he and fellow teachers discreetly guide the student from teacher to teacher. This method helps a student feel less stress and have a better school experience.

Other strategies involve the teacher modifying a small aspect of the classroom with the benefit extending to the entire class. One teacher tells about how he now gives all of his students an activity when waiting for another assignment or another activity. This decrease in unstructured time has resulted in fewer disciplinary problems. Many students, including those with Asperger Syndrome, have difficulty with unstructured periods.

This book gives methods that can help any teacher make simple accommodations for a student with Asperger Syndrome. A teacher does not need a special degree in order to teach students with this disorder effectively. Students with Asperger Syndrome respond favorably to adults who care about them and are willing to try different approaches to helping them. As with any student, a student with Asperger Syndrome can tell if a teacher feels frustrated and whether or not the teacher likes him. The use of simple and effective techniques can help teachers overcome their own anxiety and frustrations associated with teaching students with Asperger Syndrome. Many of the suggestions made in this book could work well for students with other difficulties.

What is Asperger Syndrome?

Medical professionals and researchers do not know the cause of Asperger Syndrome or any of the Autism Spectrum Disorders. Afflictions such as Autism, Childhood Degenerative Disorder, Asperger Syndrome, and some other disorders fall under the umbrella of Pervasive Developmental Disorders.

Asperger Syndrome can affect an individual's nervous system and other body systems as well. Symptoms of this disorder include problems with muscle tone, gross and fine motor skills, and the body's ability to adapt to the environment (e.g. temperature, skin sensitivity). These students often do not understand simple unwritten school and social rules that other students learn without much effort. Students with Asperger Syndrome are often unable to understand abstract concepts readily. They tend to think in concrete terms.

Additionally, these students have difficulty in social situations. Since school is a very social place, and students with Asperger Syndrome usually have trouble with social relationships, school can be a very stressful environment. The school day may be eight hours long, so the student with Asperger Syndrome needs to "hold it together" for long periods. Students with Asperger Syndrome also often lack the organizational skills needed to be successful academically in school.

Medical professionals and researchers know of no cure for any of the Autism Spectrum Disorders. Additionally, researchers have not developed one particular, specific treatment method that has been shown to consistently alleviate or reduce symptoms of this disorder. For instance, certain medications work to reduce several symptoms for some students, but not for others. The severity and variety of symptoms vary. While one student may flap, or shake his hands in the air, another student with Asperger Syndrome may pace, walking back and forth.

Further, educational research on decreasing the symptoms of the disorder in the classroom does not indicate any single method that will aid all students with Asperger Syndrome. However, it should be apparent to any educator who has worked with a student with Asperger Syndrome that students with this disorder need extra support and accommodations throughout the day. These students need modifications at home, in the community, and in school to help them to be successful with daily living.

While students with Asperger Syndrome may look like "typical" students, the way in which they process information is different. These students have the same range of intelligence as other students, so some educators feel that these students should be able to travel the hallways and pass from class to class without difficulty. A teacher may feel that a student who is constantly lost in the hallways and is consistently late for class is "not trying hard enough" or is behaving badly.

Asperger Syndrome manifests itself in many different ways depending on the individual. Sometimes, symptoms of Asperger Syndrome can mimic behavioral difficulties or even stubbornness. The teacher needs to get to know the student so she can determine how to help decrease the negative symptoms of Asperger Syndrome.

Changes in routine and surprises can be difficult for these students. Students with Asperger Syndrome may need special schedules to avoid feelings of surprise that can lead to frustration and anxiety. Another characteristic of students with this disorder is that they have an impaired sensory system. This impairment means that these students process environmental stimuli differently than for typical individuals. Noises, tastes, and textures may feel more intense. Since there are a great deal of environmental stimuli in school, such as noisy hallways and odorous lunchrooms, accommodations need to be made so that students with Asperger Syndrome can feel more at ease. In order to learn effectively, students need to have their physical needs met and to feel comfortable in school.

This feeling of ease at school is the goal of the school personnel when making accommodations for students with Asperger Syndrome.

Students with Asperger Syndrome may often feel frustration in school. When a student feels frustrated, he may not learn to his fullest potential. A new lesson in mathematics may be easily within the intellectual capabilities of the student with Asperger Syndrome. However, due to a lower frustration tolerance, that student may react negatively to the lesson. Students with Asperger Syndrome may cry or tantrum when frustrated by academic subjects.

An impaired sensory system affects the student's visual-spatial capabilities, such as the ability to find certain patterns on maps, for example political boundaries. Students with Asperger Syndrome may seem confused when presented with many visual stimuli found in textbooks and other instructional resources.

Even lunchtime can be difficult for the student with Asperger Syndrome. The type of food served is often an issue for these students. It is common for students with Asperger Syndrome to have unique food preferences. These food preferences range from not eating any spicy foods to only eating a limited variety of foods. (Some students may only want to eat pizza for lunch.) Some students request that their parents or the cafeteria staff serve different foods on separate plates. In addition to unique food preferences, school cafeterias are crowded, excessively noisy, and smelly, and can result in sensory overload for the student with Asperger Syndrome.

Sometimes a teacher has difficulty understanding the need to accommodate for such a student. At times, teachers feel that they are giving the student with Asperger Syndrome an unfair advantage and that they are not preparing the student for the "real world."

Once a teacher begins to understand her student with Asperger Syndrome, she starts to realize that poor behaviors are not due to conduct problems. Instead, teachers understand that students with Asperger Syndrome behave inappropriately at times because they do not have any better coping mechanisms. Teachers who have had success with their students realize that making changes to the student's external environment often determines success or failure for the student with Asperger Syndrome.

In this book, the reader will find problems typical for students with Asperger Syndrome in the classroom and the school environment. The solutions to such problems, which are also contained in this book, originate from teachers who have experienced success with these students.

A day in the life of a student with Asperger Syndrome
By Joshua S. Betts, aged 12

Mom wakes me in the morning. My mom always is prepping me to get up and she always puts my clothes for the day on my bed. I don't get up until after she leaves my room. My mom takes me out to the bus. That's right, I'm a momma's boy.

I sit behind the bus driver because it is the easiest seat to get to. Also, when my friend Amy gets on the bus, she sees me right away so she can sit with me.

When I get to school, I walk to the locker banks and go to my locker. My locker is easy to find because it is close to the end of the locker row. I then have to input my super-secret government F.B.I. code that only I know, I think. Then I take off my backpack and get my binder out.

Homeroom (a brief period of class time at the beginning and end of the school day) is up the dreaded stairs. Homeroom is a chance to relax and talk to friends. The teacher keeps it quiet.

Technology education is usually my next class. I like it. The teacher is pretty nice. I like the activities that we engage in, such as building a bridge, and seeing how many pounds it can carry.

Next comes math. Ugh. I know I'll need to know math for my future as a video-game programmer (yes, I have geeky dreams). Math is a little boring. At least I'm doing well on my report card. I'll admit that I take special education math (blushing).

Then there's reading where I "rock." It's basically reading very interesting chapter books (books with chapters). There is a very nice teacher. It's not special education.

Then there is lunch, one of my favorite subjects! We can eat and talk to our friends, and eat some more. It's not loud for me, so don't worry.

The food is pretty good. My mom used to make my lunch. I used to only eat a carrot, potato chips, and a surprise, like chocolate. Now, I am eating a greater variety of foods. I can stomach the school lunch that includes pizza on Fridays, chicken strips, and other, um, interesting foods.

Science is one of the best subjects because it is so fun, fun, fun. It is my favorite time of the day. The teacher is fun and funny. The projects are fun and occasionally funny. The teacher really understands me. He knows how to make complicated subjects easy. He also jokes with kids.

We have a special time of day in which we get help with homework and study. It's at the end of the day. It is very helpful to get organized.

I do have an aide for some of the day. She tries to stop me from flapping. Since I have a short attention span, and because she likes me, she usually helps me find where I am supposed to be in my books during class. She gives me free back scratches when I feel all flappy (when I feel like clapping my hands together).

Usually I goof around with friends on the way to the bus. I'm happy that I'm finally able to go home. You could say that we have a mini-celebration every day. When I get home, I take off my backpack and ask my mom for a snack. I play some video games until my mom says that we have to do homework.

School is better now than it used to be. I'm handling the school day better, and I don't need an aide as much. My teachers are all trying to help, and I appreciate it.

CHAPTER 1

"Doing" School

Typically, students learn to "do" school by watching others and taking directions from adults. There are many unwritten rules and procedures that all students need to follow.

Students need to understand these rules to be successful at school. For instance, most students know without being taught that they may not stand up in the middle of a class and make noise. Most students also know not to stare out the window and hum during class. In addition, students know that, even though they may be bored, they should not yawn loudly. Students learn this information by watching classmates and from non-verbal messages communicated by the teacher. A teacher's scornful look at a classmate who talks out of turn sends a strong message to most school students to wait until the teacher calls on them.

"Doing" school involves performing numerous actions that the majority of students automatically understand. "Doing" school includes attending to tasks and following the teacher's directions regarding assignments, standing in line, and putting away materials. Additionally, students need to understand the regular activities of the school day including talking appropriately with teachers and classmates and following the "norms" of the school.

Students with Asperger Syndrome can benefit from explicit instruction and direction in all aspects of their school experiences. These students also need to understand exactly what behaviors the teachers and school staff expect from them during the school day. These students can learn to perform these behaviors appropriately with instruction, guidance, and having simple accommodations made for them.

Helping the student get from place to place

Transitional periods may be the hardest part of the day for students with Asperger Syndrome. Douglas, a middle-school (grades 6–8) teacher, used a few simple methods to help Justin, a student with Asperger Syndrome, during transition periods. He gave Justin a few minutes before and after instruction to organize his materials. This extra time helped to reduce Justin's feelings of rushing when he had to switch classes. Douglas also positioned Justin's desk near the door so that he would have easier access to the exit.

In addition, Douglas wrote assignments for the next day on the board at the beginning of the class period as opposed to the end of class. By doing this, Douglas reassured Justin that he had enough time to write his assignment in his book.

When it was time to change classes, Douglas stood at the door and said, "Goodbye, Justin. Do you know where you're going?" This personalized attention permitted Justin to have the added support he needed. Douglas also requested that Justin's other teachers stand at their door to "retrieve" Justin.

Douglas' method of passing his student from class to class only takes a small amount of time and can greatly benefit the student with Asperger Syndrome. Some teachers report that the use of a peer helper in hallways has been useful for students with Asperger Syndrome. A peer helper can walk with the student to help him navigate the school building and even assist in carrying materials if needed.

Summary of strategies

1. Place the desk of the student with Asperger Syndrome near the classroom door.

2. Allow enough time at the end of class for the students to get themselves organized and put their books away before the next class.

3. Stand at the door to assist the student in exiting and entering classrooms.

4.   Have other teachers stand at their doors to help guide the student with Asperger Syndrome into their classrooms.

5.   Use a peer helper to help guide the student with Asperger Syndrome.

Points for reflection

1.   What are other ways that a teacher can help a student with Asperger Syndrome navigate the school environment?

2.   What other accommodations can you make that will not affect the student's instructional time?

Peer helpers

Many students are happy to help a peer in need. Peers can be very effective with the process of helping students navigate hallways and classrooms in school. A student with Asperger Syndrome may use a peer helper daily or on an occasional basis.

Some teachers, like Steve, a high-school science teacher, have provided an informal "training" for peer helpers. Steve has a student named Mark who has Asperger Syndrome. Mark's peers receive training to learn about Asperger Syndrome. As part of the training, Mark's peer helpers listen to an explanation about symptoms of Asperger Syndrome to help the students understand Mark better. Appendix B provides a sample worksheet that teachers can use when training peer helpers. The teacher can easily modify the worksheet to fit the needs of the peer helpers and the student with Asperger Syndrome.

Steve introduced the idea of peer helpers to Mark and his parents. Steve discussed this issue first with Mark's parents. Some families may not be receptive to another student knowing that their child has a disability. Sometimes a peer helper may not be a good option. For example, some students may be embarrassed having other students help them.

To select a peer helper, Steve chose students with whom Mark was already familiar and friendly. Some teachers suggest waiting for a few weeks after school begins to see if natural relationships form before selecting peer helpers. For a responsible, friendly student, being a peer helper can be an honor. The peer helper should not view his or her role as "babysitting" for the student with Asperger Syndrome. It is important, however, that the teacher choose a good match for the student with this disorder. The teacher needs to consider the personalities of all the students in the classroom before choosing a peer helper.

Sally, a fifth-grade teacher, knew a student in her classroom who would be a good match for Jared, a student with Asperger Syndrome. She picked a student who she thought would be able to handle the extra responsibility of helping Jared. Prior to the beginning of the school year, Sally called the potential peer helper's parents. She talked with them and then the student about this role. Sally explained to the parents and student about the symptoms of Asperger Syndrome. This way, the peer helper would be able to understand and be patient with Jared's behaviors. After communicating with the parents and student, Sally felt confident that she had made a good match.

This peer helper would assist Jared to travel from class to class and help him find his way to lunch and breaks. The peer helper would not have to sit next to the student during classes unless he chose to.

Sally's preparation for making Jared feel comfortable in her class and in school was successful. She kept a close watch on Jared for the first few days of school and frequently asked him how he felt and if he needed more help. If Jared did request help with something, such as with following his schedule, Sally would address his problems promptly and ease Jared's stress. Many times, the peer helper asked Jared for some minor assistance.

Summary of strategies

1.   Carefully assess which students will be peer helpers.

2.   Ask the parents of the peer helper for permission to use him or her in this role.

3.   Provide a short "training" for peer helpers.

Points for reflection

1. Why may a student feel embarrassed by having a peer helper?

2. What activities or roles may be inappropriate for the peer helper?

3. What kind of personality would fit well with the role of peer helper?

Getting to know the school

Most teachers are excited and happy to start a new school year. Many teachers enjoy discovering the students' personalities and the challenge of teaching many different types of students. Teachers also usually feel some anxiety as they anticipate the process of gathering information about their new students to help the students learn in the most productive way possible. Students have similar feelings of excitement and anxiety.

Mary, an elementary-school (kindergarten to grade 5) teacher, did not want to have the same experience as one of her colleagues had in the previous year. During that year, on the first week of school, Thomas, a student with Asperger Syndrome, had several "meltdowns." Thomas cried and kept repeating that he did not know what to do. The other students quickly learned where to place their coats and bookbags, and the names of their teachers. They also understood their "jobs" for the day, and organized their books and papers.

Mary learned that she was to have a new student who has Asperger Syndrome. His name is Frank. Mary read about Asperger Syndrome and thought that she needed to use some strategies to make sure that Frank's school year started well. Mary consulted her colleagues who worked with students with Asperger Syndrome. She also read a great deal about interventions for students with Autism Spectrum Disorders.

Mary contacted Frank's parents about visiting the school before the school year began. During their visit, Mary pointed out the particular places in the classroom that would be important to Frank. Mary showed Frank his place for his coat, bookbag, and lunch (his "cubby"). Mary picked Frank's cubby to be at the end of the row. The location of the cubby gave Frank more space to move. Mary also gave Frank a map of the room.

Mary walked Frank through the cafeteria lunch line so he would know the routine and feel less anxious at lunch. It is important that students feel comfortable during lunch so they will have an appetite, eat, and have energy for the remainder of their day.

Mary also had Frank's desk organized. Frank sat at the desk to see if he liked its positioning and placement in the classroom. It is a good idea for the teacher to consider the following factors when determining the desk placement for a student with Asperger Syndrome: the proximity to the other students in the classroom, the distance from the chalkboard, and possible distractions from the hallway. Mary placed an information sheet on Frank's desk so he could glance at it if he needed to check his schedule or needed materials for an assignment.

Mary listened to Frank's feedback about the location of the desk. He was happy that it was placed at the end of the aisle. Mary then took Frank and his parents on a short tour of the school. She showed them all the areas that Frank would use, such as the lunchroom, gym, art room, music room, bathroom, school lobby, and hallways. Additionally, Mary provided Frank with another map, which showed the school hallways and classrooms. Mary also took digital pictures of each location so Frank could study these pictures at home.

Mary's orientation helped Frank and his family understand his schedule and what would be required of him during the day. Students with Asperger Syndrome usually need information ahead of time to give them an opportunity to let such information "sink in." This advance planning can make the process of adjusting to a new environment much easier on the student.

Student information form

The authors suggest that teachers collect student information at the beginning of the school year and when a student with Asperger Syndrome starts at a new school. Appendix C is a sample student infor-mation form that teachers can use to assess the student's interests, sensitivities, and preferences. The teacher and school staff can refer to the completed form throughout the school year. School personnel can also give the form to staff as a reminder regarding the reason that the student needs certain accommodations. The teacher or aide will need to update the form as the student develops.

Summary of strategies

1. Allow the student with Asperger Syndrome to visit the classroom to get familiar with the layout of the room several times before the start of the school year.

2. Give the student a map of the room and a schedule so that he knows what to expect during the school day.

3. Let the student visit all the important places in the school so he becomes familiar with them.

4. Listen to feedback that the student provides regarding the location of his desk so the student can be as comfortable as possible.

5. Use a peer helper to assist the student in becoming familiar with the classroom and school routines.

6. Use a student information form to collect valuable information about the individual characteristics of the student (see Appendix C).

Points for reflection

1. If you have taught a student with Asperger Syndrome, how did you feel on learning that the student had this disorder?

2. How would you help a student with Asperger Syndrome orient to your classroom and to school requirements?

Stairs and other physical demands

Since students with Asperger Syndrome often have low muscle tone and decreased muscle strength, these students have difficulty navigating the stairs. Sometimes, the amount of physical activity is a reason why students with Asperger Syndrome dislike school. One teacher, Billy, discovered this one day when he took a student with Asperger Syndrome, Dan, with him on the elevator.

Apparently, Dan went home and told his parents that he had a great day. When his parents asked Dan what made his day so wonderful, Dan replied that he was able to ride the elevator instead of trudging up and down the steps.

After hearing how much Dan liked riding the elevator, Billy arranged that Dan continue to use the elevator. When the teachers were deciding on Dan's schedule, they tried to put him in as many classes as they could on the same floor, to minimize the need for traveling up and down the steps.

Students with Asperger Syndrome may have a hard time traveling the steps while holding the books that they need to carry from class to class. Billy had observed Dan on the stairs between classes and observed that Dan traveled very slowly on the steps and that he did not seem to balance well. Billy was also concerned that students would push Dan on the steps because the steps were so crowded. The principal gave Dan a special exception and permitted him to use a bookbag throughout the day. By using the bookbag, Dan had his hands free to hold stair railings. Billy arranged to have Dan keep an extra set of books at home so that he did not have to carry his books to and from school.

Some teachers have a peer helper assigned to a student to assist with carrying materials. However, teachers have also said that they try to keep the student as independent as possible and encourage the student to carry some of his own books.

Summary of strategies

1.   If possible and necessary, have the student use an elevator.

2.   Allow the student to have an extra set of books at home to reduce the need for carrying so many materials to and from school.

3.   If necessary, use a peer helper to help carry items around school.

Points for reflection

1.   How do you balance helping a student with Asperger Syndrome learn to be independent while at the same time providing added supports for the student?

2.   What suggestions might you make to help a student with Asperger Syndrome to travel along long hallways in school?

Schedules

A simple schedule can help the student with Asperger Syndrome feel more at ease in the school environment. A schedule allows these students to know the daily routine and know in advance what events will be happening.

Schedules can help students with Asperger Syndrome in both elementary school and higher grades. In elementary school, the students are usually with one teacher the whole day. However, they usually leave the classroom for lunch, special classes, and assemblies.

Carole, a third-grade teacher, noticed that Pam, a student with Asperger Syndrome, had difficulty remembering what class came next during her school day. Pam became flustered at times because she could not remember what books she needed to take out of her desk for the next class.

To help Pam, Carole pasted a schedule to the top of Pam's desk. Carole used clear lettering for the schedule and kept it simple. She did not put in clock times for classes. Carole merely showed how the day would unfold for Pam by listing the sequence of classes and activities in order of their occurrence.

On days when there was a special event, Carole made sure Pam knew there would be a change in the schedule. Carole also sent a note home to the parents when there would be a special event, so the parents could remind Pam about the change in schedule before school. Carole also routinely sent home a monthly calendar to Pam's parents noting any changes in the routine school day. Carole found that when Pam knew in advance about the change she was much more comfortable with the change in schedule. Carole also noticed that by having a schedule at Pam's desk, Pam was more organized.

If the child has difficulty reading, picture schedules may be used. Even after the student can read, picture schedules may still be useful. The teacher will need to assess the personality of the student to determine which type of schedule will work best.

In most middle schools, students go from class to class for all of their school day. Each change of class is a transition, and requires a new set of books and rules for each teacher. These transitions can be worrisome for students without difficulties, but for a student that has Asperger Syndrome these transitions can become traumatic.

Jeremy, a ten-year-old student with Asperger Syndrome, worried about switching classes and getting lost in middle school. When he started at the middle school, Jeremy was given a standard schedule, but he could not follow it. Jeremy's teacher, Sandra, heard from another teacher that visual cues can help students with Asperger Syndrome.

Sandra decided to take a digital picture of each of Jeremy's teachers standing next to the door of their classroom. She also took pictures of the lunchroom, the break area, the bathroom area, and all other areas of the school. Using a computer, Sandra made the pictures smaller and printed them in the order of Jeremy's daily schedule. Sandra placed the schedule in the front cover of Jeremy's binder. The schedule was not noticeable to other students. Sandra and the other teachers did not want to call attention to Jeremy's differences. Since the picture schedule was easy to follow, Jeremy knew where his next class was located. His anxiety regarding becoming lost decreased.

Summary of strategies

1. Paste a schedule to the top of a student's desk so the student can frequently glance at it.

2. Send the parents a note so they can help the student remember any schedule changes.

3. Take pictures of the places where the student needs to go during his school day and make a visual schedule for the student.

4. Give plenty of verbal and written notice when there is a "special event."

Points for reflection

1. Does a daily schedule help you to feel more comfortable navigating your day?

2. What other types of schedules might be effective for students with Asperger Syndrome?

Wait times

There is a great deal of wait time in school. Students need to wait for the next activity in classes, wait in line to go the cafeteria, and wait for buses. These unstructured periods are difficult for students with Asperger Syndrome. Often, students do not know how to occupy themselves during "wait times."

Jake was a student with Asperger Syndrome who had difficulty during these times. Whenever Jake had to wait for anything, and when there was no assigned task, Jake would begin to flap and make car-like noises. This behavior was very distracting and annoying to the other students. If the teacher told Jake to stop making the gestures and sounds, he would begin to pull on other students' bodies or bookbags.

Mike was a middle-school teacher who had Jake in his homeroom class. He also saw Jake at the end of the day when it was time for the students to organize themselves to get ready to go home. Mike saw Jake start to flap and make noises during the wait times and thought that it was important to find something for Jake to do during this time. Mike tried to think of something that would occupy Jake during these times.

Mike recalled a technique that used "wait boxes" for students with Autism Spectrum Disorders. Mike decided he would try to make a "wait box" for Jake. Mike found out what were Jake's favorite magazine, toys, and hobbies. Mike obtained many of Jake's favorite items, such as plastic building blocks, books, and magazines, and placed these objects in a small box. Whenever Mike stopped class, or asked the students to wait a moment to get in line for lunch, he would simply prompt Jake to use any items that he chose from his "wait box."

After a while, Mike only needed to say "break time" and Jake would reach for items in his wait box. This technique continues to help Jake get through break times with a minimum of flapping and noise making.

Summary of strategies

1.   Gather items that the student with Asperger Syndrome enjoys, such as books, puzzles, or small toys, to make a "wait box."

Point for reflection

1.   What other activities or materials might be used to help a student get through unstructured times during the school day?

Lockers

Many students with Asperger Syndrome have difficulty manipulating small objects. In addition, these students often have fine motor skill problems. They may have difficulty grasping small items in their hands as well as their peers do.

Given these physical difficulties, the use of lockers may present a problem for students with Asperger Syndrome. Lockers often have combination locks. These require some finger dexterity. Other lockers have locks that are opened with small keys.

The space between each locker is often very small and the locker bank can become noisy and crowded. The student with Asperger Syndrome may feel sensory overload. He needs to cope with loud noises, to be in close proximity to other students, and to organize his materials.

Jason is a student with Asperger Syndrome. Jeff, a high-school teacher and Jason's homeroom teacher, decided that he had to find a way to help Jason access his locker quickly and easily. He gave Jason a locker at the very end of the row of lockers. Jeff chose the location of the locker so Jason could find his locker easily and have a little extra space. This would reduce the likelihood that nearby students would jostle Jason. Ideally, Jeff would have liked to have one locker empty next to Jason for more added space, but this was not feasible due to the number of students at the school.

Jason had difficulty manipulating the combination due to his problem with fine motor skills. Jeff made sure that Jason had a keyed lock instead. Jason found the keyed lock easier to use. Jason was given this key on a key chain, which could be fastened to his belt. Each day, when Jason got home, his mother took the key and key chain and put it into Jason's binder. Each morning during homeroom, Jeff reminded Jason to fasten the key chain to his belt or belt loop on his pants.

To help Jason to remember what books he needed for his classes, Jeff put a color-coded schedule in Jason's locker. He placed coordinating color codes on the spines of each of Jason's books and notebooks. Therefore, Jason only had to look at the color of the next class he would go to, and find the same color books in his locker. By using this system, Jason could find the books quickly and get to class on time.

Summary of strategies

1.   Give the student as much space as possible between lockers.

2.   Try to place the student's locker at the end of a row, where there is a little more room to move around.

3. Use a key and lock or keypad instead of a combination lock if this is easier for the student to use.

Points for reflection

1. What alternatives may be used instead of lockers for a student with Asperger Syndrome?

2. Can you think of other methods to help a student access his locker quickly and easily?

School bus

Riding the school bus can be an extremely noisy, cramped, and bumpy experience. The school bus is a place where there are many students and not much adult supervision. Many students enjoy the stimulation and freedom of the bus ride, since these rides can be a fun place to talk with friends. However, many students with Asperger Syndrome, who have difficulty in social relationships and who often have impaired sensory systems, find that the school bus environment is over-stimulating and uncomfortable.

Dave, a middle-school teacher, heard that Ryan, a student of his with Asperger Syndrome, received disciplinary referrals to the principal from the bus driver for yelling and getting into fights on the school bus. Dave realized after speaking to the bus driver that the driver did not know that Ryan has Asperger Syndrome.

The driver and principal did not understand that Ryan's behavior on the bus may be due to symptoms of Asperger Syndrome, and not intentional misconduct. Dave thought he needed to take action, in part because he did not want the school staff to label Ryan a troublemaker.

Dave talked to the bus driver and principal and informed them about the symptoms prevalent in Asperger Syndrome. Dave explained that the disorder is a medical condition that affects a student's body and sensory system. Dave also explained that a student with Asperger Syndrome may become agitated when overwhelmed with sensory input (such as from noise and social interactions).

Dave, the bus driver, and the principal, came up with a simple plan for Ryan. Ryan was assigned a seat behind the bus driver. Ryan chose to sit by himself. He liked the idea that he did not have to interact with anyone on the bus if he did not want to. The bus driver agreed to have the radio turned off during the bus ride. Additionally, the driver began to greet Ryan with a smile whenever he entered the bus, and said "Goodbye" when he exited the bus. After some investigation, Dave discovered that there were students on the bus who teased Ryan. The driver and principal talked to these students about bullying and gave stern warnings that their taunting behaviors needed to stop immediately. The principal explained to these students that Ryan needed to have a quieter and calmer school bus ride.

Dave's actions were successful, and Ryan had no more disciplinary referrals from the bus driver. Ryan felt better about going to school on the school bus. Instead of appearing upset each morning when he arrived at school, Ryan seemed calm. Ryan's school day began much better with a quieter bus ride. Dave's strategy worked because it reduced the sensory stimulation with which Ryan had to cope. Additionally, a personal relationship between Ryan and the bus driver developed.

Summary of strategies

1. Tell the bus driver and principal that the student has Asperger Syndrome. Educate these individuals about the symptoms and behaviors associated with Asperger Syndrome.

2. Decrease the volume of the radio on the bus if noise is a problem for the student.

3. Let the student with Asperger Syndrome sit directly behind the bus driver to minimize stress.

4. Ask the bus driver to smile and acknowledge the student when he enters and exits the bus.

5. Inform the bus driver about the actions to take if the student with Asperger Syndrome has a behavior problem.

Points for reflection

1. Many people do not realize that the bus ride to school can be extremely stressful for a student with Asperger Syndrome and can directly affect his school performance. Consider the ways that the bus ride can be difficult for any student and especially for a student with Asperger Syndrome.

2. Would it be more beneficial for the parents of the student with Asperger Syndrome to drive the student to school?

Homework

Writing is a challenge for many students with Asperger Syndrome. Asperger Syndrome often affects the muscular system. Poor muscle tone and deficits in fine and gross motor abilities are common. Many students with Asperger Syndrome have great difficulty writing because of these symptoms.

Schoolwork and homework require a great deal of writing. The school day is very demanding for most students, and for students with Asperger Syndrome following the rules and expectations of the school day is exhausting. While educational research is inconclusive about the benefits of homework on academic achievement, homework assignments have become a cultural norm in schools. Homework also affords students an opportunity to finish incomplete assignments and to gain extra practice. Although homework does have its advantages, the process of having to spend extra time on schoolwork and write lengthy assignments causes much stress for the student with Asperger Syndrome.

Often the student may feel so overwhelmed by the homework assignments that he begins to perseverate, loses concentration, and refuses to complete any task. The process of completing homework can become very exhausting and frustrating for the student and the parents. In addition, the student often feels like he has no chance to relax while he is at home. The tension can build to the point that the student feels he has no place to unwind and this can result in a meltdown. In summary, the student with Asperger Syndrome usually needs modifications in homework assignments because of the exhausting school day and the difficulty completing written assignments.

Barb, a high-school social studies teacher, used homework as a way to expand her students' knowledge of the subject matter. Her assignments required students to do investigations using the computer and to write reports on current events.

Barb believed that effective teachers get to know their students' strengths and weaknesses and try to help each student achieve his or her very best. Barb knew many of her students on a personal level. Her students seemed to like and respect her.

Barb understood a little about Asperger Syndrome, but said that she was no expert. However, she wanted to know enough about Asperger Syndrome to be an effective teacher. Barb felt particularly challenged the year she had Tyler, a student with Asperger Syndrome, in her class. She had never had to deal with students having difficulty with the homework she gave them. Instead, her students liked the independence that she gave them with the assignments.

Tyler's parents helped him with homework whenever they could, but his father worked long hours and his mother had four younger siblings to manage after school. Tyler stopped doing his homework. His mother felt increasingly frustrated with the homework situation. She called Barb to get help in this regard. Barb believed that Tyler could do the homework, but that he needed some modifications.

Barb decided that much of Tyler's dislike and stress from homework came from the amount of writing that the assignments required. Barb told Tyler that instead of having to write assignments and complete worksheets, he could check off answer choices. He also began to tape-record his responses on a tape recorder for lengthy responses. For example, Barb assigned one homework project where the students had to explain how the news about a recent jump in gas prices related to the concept of inflation, which the students had discussed and defined in class. The simple accommodation of using a tape recorder drastically altered Tyler's attitude toward this assignment and other homework.

Additionally, Barb permitted Tyler and the other students to use word-processing software and print written reports. Barb tried to avoid making the requirements less stringent for Tyler because he had the academic capability to complete all the coursework. However, Barb sometimes reduced the workload for Tyler if he became overwhelmed. Barb also notified Tyler's mother that she may help him with the writing and typing of his assignments and that she could modify the homework herself at home, if she felt it was necessary. These changes have been very positive for Tyler and have both reduced his stress level and made school a more enjoyable place for him. Barb felt that she was not lowering the standards of her curriculum by modifying Tyler's assignments. Instead, she was helping him achieve his full potential.

Several teachers say that a homework sheet is effective in reminding students to complete homework assignments. Appendix A provides an example of a homework sheet.

Summary of strategies

1. Allow the student to have his homework load decreased, if he is doing well academically and does not need to do as much homework as others.

2. Ask the student's parent to scribe the homework to reduce the amount of writing that need to be completed.

3. Give notice of tests and projects as far in advance as possible so the student with Asperger Syndrome can plan his time accordingly.

4. Involve the parents with the process as much as possible, as their support is imperative to the student's homework success.

5. Allow the student to use the computer for writing assignments as much as possible.

6. Use a daily homework checklist (see Appendix A) to help the student organize his homework and know what items he needs to bring home.

Points for reflection

1.   Consider the reason why you assign homework. If a student with Asperger Syndrome finds homework extremely stressful, would you be reluctant to decrease the amount of homework?

2.   Do you feel that it is fair for the student with Asperger Syndrome to receive less homework than other students are given?

Organization of assignments

Many students with Asperger Syndrome have one common area of difficulty that involves organization. If these students do not receive assistance, their desks are often covered with paper that has been crumpled or thrown about. These students lose pencils, miss assignments, and misplace library books. The continual loss of items and assignments leads to the student with Asperger Syndrome feeling like a failure and lowering his self-confidence.

Warren is an elementary-school teacher who took an interest in Jonah, a student with Asperger Syndrome. Jonah continually lost things. He would misplace his personal items, such as his coat, gym clothes, and lunch bag. He also misplaced assignments and other papers. Jonah could not find anything in his desk and was constantly searching for lost items. Much of Jonah's class time was taken up by his disorganization. Jonah could not focus on the lesson because he was always worried about things that he could not find. Jonah's mother frequently contacted Warren for help in finding items that Jonah had misplaced.

Warren felt frustrated with the current situation and knew that he needed to find a way to help Jonah organize himself and his belongings. Warren learned in a teaching workshop that students with Autism Spectrum Disorders have trouble with organization. Since Warren had talent in drawing and art, he thought about using these skills to create some solutions to the problem of Jonah losing his belongings. Warren was acutely aware that Jonah was quite sensitive about not wanting to appear "different" from other students. Warren needed to devise a solution that would not single out Jonah from the other students.

Warren knew that verbal directions did not usually help Jonah, so he decided to try using diagrams and drawings to assist him. Warren drew a small diagram for Jonah showing him where to place his books, papers, and writing instruments in his desk. This diagram was laminated and placed inside Jonah's desk.

Warren also thought that other students could also benefit from additional organizational reminders that he could place throughout the classroom. Warren drew pictures that he posted next to the students' coat and bookbag closet. The pictures showed the students where their personal items should be placed in their cubbies. Soon, Warren had made a number of organizational guides that were located throughout the classroom for all students to view. Warren found that the guides helped all the students become more responsible for their own materials and their assignments.

Additionally, Warren noticed that Jonah did not remember the location of his desk or cubby as easily as the other students did. Warren clearly posted the students' names on their desks and left these tags on the desks for the entire class year, even though he knew the other students did not need the tags after the first few weeks of school. In this way, Warren did not make Jonah feel different from the other students. Warren made Jonah's nametag on his cubby a little different, with brighter colors, so Jonah could find the cubby easily. He also placed Jonah's cubby at the beginning of the row.

In time, Jonah became more independent and was able to manage his books and supplies with little direction from Warren. Warren was glad that he was able to help Jonah without drawing undue attention to Jonah's disorder.

In the higher grades, several other aids can help a child with Asperger Syndrome organize his assignments. Each student should have an agenda book where he writes down the assignments for his different classes. The teacher for each class should be sure to write the assignments on the board, as the student with Asperger Syndrome may miss writing down the assignment if the teacher gives the assignment verbally. The student with Asperger Syndrome may be distracted when the teacher is talking and will miss the assignment completely.

For a long-term project, the teacher can send home a rubric for all the students that breaks down exactly when the assignment is due and what needs to be done to obtain a certain grade. By using this rubric, the student with Asperger Syndrome will have concise, clear directions in front of him when he is at home trying to figure out the assignment. Using the rubric, the student can also decide what material he will need for the project in advance. He can then enlist the help of his parents. The key idea for the teachers is to recognize that these students lack organizational skills and to anticipate how the lack of these skills will affect their schoolwork and homework.

Jasmine is a student who is intelligent and verbal and has Asperger Syndrome. She has a definite problem with organizing and often will miss an assignment because it is not written down in her agenda book. She also cannot explain to her mother, who monitors her daily assignments, what she needs to do for homework. Rachel, who is Jasmine's homeroom teacher, decided to create an organization system after Jasmine's mother called her and said that Jasmine had been missing assignments at school and her grades were suffering.

Rachel gave Jasmine a special assignment book and made sure that Jasmine knew how to use it. Rachel met with each of Jasmine's teachers and told them that they needed to write the assignments in the upper left corner of the board so that Jasmine would know where to look for the daily homework.

Rachel also requested that each teacher announce what the assignment was about five minutes prior to the class ending. This announcement enabled students to have enough time to copy down assignments in the agenda book. Rachel also requested that each teacher give at least one week notice of any test and that the teacher include in the assignments the date of the test. In this way, Jasmine and her parents would have advance notice of the test and Jasmine's parents could help her prepare for the test.

Each day, all the students returned to Rachel's homeroom for last period. During this period, Rachel made sure that Jasmine's agenda book was up to date. If Jasmine had missed an assignment, Rachel called the teacher to clarify the exact directions of the homework. Additionally, Rachel checked Jasmine's handwriting to insure that it was legible so her parents would be able to read the agenda book. The checking at the end of the day proved invaluable to both Jasmine and her parents, and Jasmine turned her assignments in on time.

Later in the school year, Rachel decided to try to see if Jasmine could take more responsibility for planning what homework she needed to do nightly. Rachel developed a daily homework checklist that Jasmine completed at the end of the day (see Appendix A). At first, Rachel had to go slowly over each item on the checklist with Jasmine. Gradually, Jasmine became more independent and learned to fill in the checklist on her own. Although Jasmine did not become totally self-sufficient regarding her organization and homework, Rachel's strategies helped Jasmine become more aware of the necessity of organization.

The other method that Rachel used to help Jasmine was to get Jasmine a large binder that she carried with her throughout the school day. This binder was used to put in all papers that were completed and all notes for each subject, and also had a place for homework, papers to go home, and a pocket for small reading books. Since the binder had a place for each subject, Jasmine knew where to file her papers after each class. This organization system worked well for Jasmine because it was simple to use. Additionally, Jasmine understood the importance of not losing any papers.

Occasionally, Rachel used a different method to receive Jasmine's lengthy written assignments. Jasmine's mother emailed these lengthy assignments directly to Rachel to ensure that the work was delivered on time. Previously, Jasmine lost several assignments prior to handing them to Rachel.

Summary of strategies

1. Use a diagram to show elementary students with Asperger Syndrome where to put items in their desk.

2. Place the students' names clearly on their desks and other areas. This way, all students can easily locate their desks and belongings.

3.   Remind the student to fill out a daily agenda book for assignments.

4.   Request that all teachers write the assignments down in a similar place on the board so the student can see the assignment and copy it into his agenda book.

5.   Ask the teachers to give as much advance notice as possible to the students for tests and long-term projects.

6.   Check the assignment book at the end of the day to make sure it is accurate and legible.

7.   Use a daily homework checklist for the student to foster independence (see Appendix A).

8.   Use a large binder to keep all papers in their proper place during the school day and encourage the student to file the papers immediately after class to keep the papers organized and available.

9.   In the elementary levels, draw pictures near the students' cubbies to show where the students should put their coats and bookbags.

Points for reflection

1.   Do you feel that helping a student organize his materials should be part of a teacher's duties?

2.   Do you feel that schools would benefit from teaching organization skills? How could you implement this in your school?

Fire drills

Fire drills are unpredictable and noisy. The crowds of students in a fire drill move quickly. Students with Asperger Syndrome have trouble with inconsistency and changes in routine. These students may have trouble in crowds due to the noise level and the unpredictability of the movement of individuals.

Lori is a fifth-grade teacher. She knew that a fire drill was planned for later during the week. Knowing that Leon, a student with Asperger Syndrome, has trouble with immediate changes to routine, Lori decided to help Leon cope effectively with the fire drill. She remembered noticing Leon crying during a fire drill the previous school year.

Lori obtained permission from her principal to inform Leon ahead of time about the drill. She also broke down the procedures that would occur during the drill into steps. She wrote down these steps and explained them to Leon. Lori suggested that Leon hold his ears during the drill and made sure that he understood exactly what he needed to do during the drill. Lori told Leon that in the future no one would tell Leon about these drills, so he needed to spend some time memorizing the steps he would have to take during the drills.

Leon has had successful fire drill experiences since Lori helped him. He no longer needs to refer to the written steps that he needs to take during drills. Leon takes fire drills seriously. He explained to new students what the procedures are during the drills. Lori noticed that Leon has not been the only student to hold his ears during fire drills. She also thinks that all her students could benefit from staff directly teaching the steps that the students need to take during these drills.

Summary of strategies

1. Teach students with Asperger Syndrome the procedures that need to take place during a fire drill. Write these procedures down for the student to review.

2. Allow the student an opportunity to practice these skills by giving advance notice of at least one fire drill.

3. Allow the student to hold his ears, use earplugs, or use other adaptations to reduce the chance that the student will become upset during a fire drill.

Points for reflection

1.   How do you feel during simulated or real emergencies?

2.   What has helped you to deal effectively with these situations?

Fieldtrips

Although most students look forward to fieldtrips as a break in their routine, students with Asperger Syndrome may dread fieldtrips. Sometimes students request that they be able to stay home from school on these days. This way, they do not have to worry about the change and being in a different routine and a new environment. With the proper preparation, fieldtrips can be interesting and fun for the student with Asperger Syndrome.

Avery was an elementary-school teacher who had a student with Asperger Syndrome called John. Although John had a very mild form of Asperger Syndrome, he still needed the structure of the school day to feel comfortable. Avery knew that John would be worried about the upcoming fieldtrip, but she also knew that he could participate in the trip and that it would be a good educational experience for him. This particular trip was to a museum. Avery announced the fieldtrip one week in advance. She also provided a schedule that the students would follow for that day. She taped the schedule for the fieldtrip day on John's desk so he could look at it frequently during the upcoming week.

Avery also sent John's parents, along with the permission slip, a similar schedule. She assigned John a chaperone who would only have one other student. Avery contacted the chaperone prior to the fieldtrip to let her know about John and his need for structure and routine. She made sure that this chaperone had the fieldtrip schedule.

Avery picked a student with whom John was friendly to be his buddy for the trip. She assigned only John and his friend to the chaperone, to keep socialization issues to a minimum. Avery also thought about what the students would be doing at the museum, to make sure that there was nothing too over-stimulating for John. If she felt that something would be too much for his sensory system, she would have permitted John and the chaperone to go to another exhibit instead.

Avery sent home reminders with her students one day before the fieldtrip. She reviewed the schedule with them. John's mother had also contacted Avery because John was telling her that he did not want to go on the trip. However, Avery reassured John's mother that she had planned the trip well and that John would be fine. She explained how she was preparing John for the day. John had a successful fieldtrip and Avery felt that the advance planning was the key to helping John enjoy his day.

Rose, another elementary-school teacher, planned a fieldtrip to a museum where the students were to watch an IMAX movie about skiing. Rose knew that Brian, her student with Asperger Syndrome, refused to watch movies on a large screen because the sensory stimulation was overwhelming for him. She understood that Brian would not like an IMAX movie, but Rose still felt that he needed to go on the fieldtrip and be included in the class. Rose had an aide in the class who was going on the trip with them. She told Brian about the trip and the movie and, as she anticipated, Brian did not want to go.

Rose told Brian about her plan to let him visit the gift shop and to get a snack with the aide while the class watched the movie. She encouraged Brian to participate with the class. She did not want him to feel embarrassed or different due to his having Asperger Syndrome. Brian felt comfortable knowing that Rose would not force him to see the movie, and he was actually looking forward to the trip.

Leah is a fourth-grade teacher. Jamal is a student with Asperger Syndrome. Leah found a successful accommodation for Jamal for a trip to the planetarium.

She knew that Jamal did not enjoy sitting in dark places or going to the movies. Leah told Jamal and the rest of the class about the proposed trip to the planetarium. She talked to Jamal privately and reassured him that if he felt overwhelmed by viewing the stars and planets, he could leave the planetarium for a while. She also told him that although the class would be in the planetarium for about an hour, there would be only about ten minutes in which it would be dark.

Leah stated that she felt Jamal would be able to participate for ten minutes looking at the stars. After she sent him back to his seat, she announced to the class that they had ten minutes until lunch. Leah set a large timer and had the class do some class work until the timer rang and it was time for lunch. She took Jamal aside and asked him if he would be able to sit in the planetarium for a similar length of time. Jamal said that he definitely could because now he knew what ten minutes felt like. He brought along his wristwatch to check this ten-minute interval when it was dark in the planetarium. Jamal had a successful and enjoyable trip.

Summary of strategies

1. Make a schedule for the fieldtrip.

2. Introduce the idea of the fieldtrip well in advance.

3. Send the schedule home for the parents to review.

4. Assign a chaperone and give the chaperone information about the student.

5. Assign a peer to be with the student.

6. Anticipate any sensory situations or other problems ahead of time.

7. Allow the student with Asperger Syndrome to express any questions about the trip ahead of time.

8. Explain the type of transportation and length of time it will take to get to the destination.

Points for reflection

1. Is there any way to choose a fieldtrip that would be easier for the student with Asperger Syndrome to tolerate?

2. Are there ways to allow the student with Asperger Syndrome to participate fully in the fieldtrip without the student feeling singled out for special treatment?

Assemblies

Many students with Asperger Syndrome have trouble with school assemblies. They are often noisy. Additionally, they are not within the normal school routine.

Norah was a middle-school student who has Asperger Syndrome. She disliked assemblies. She had a bad experience during one of the pep rallies when she was in fifth grade (pep rallies are events held in the school auditorium to support school sports teams). She could not stand the noise and the lights and ended up putting her hands over her ears, squeezing her eyes tightly together, and trying to crawl under her seat. After that pep rally, she avoided any type of assembly. If she knew about an assembly in advance she would beg her mother to let her miss school that day or ask her mother to pick her up early.

Jennifer, Norah's teacher, decided to help Norah tolerate assemblies better. Jennifer first gave Norah warning about a week ahead of time of the scheduled assembly. She also gave her a revised schedule for the day of the assembly. Jennifer let Norah know that she understood Norah's fear of assemblies. The next assembly was a play about pirates, presented by the fourth-grade class. Jennifer provided Norah some details about the play. She brought Norah to the auditorium and showed her where she would be sitting during the play. Jennifer had already arranged with the principal to have her class sit next to a door. This way, if Norah felt upset, she could leave easily. Jennifer suggested that Norah sit at the end of the row. On the day before the play, Jennifer told the students that the play may get a little loud at times, because of the pirates fighting, but overall the noise level should be moderate.

At the end of the day before the play, Jennifer asked Norah if she had any concerns and Norah stated that she did not have anything specific, but she hoped the play would be okay. Due to Jennifer's planning, the assembly went well for Norah. She began to feel a little overwhelmed near the end of the play, but she knew that the assembly would be over soon.

Norah was grateful that Jennifer had taken the time to accommodate her and help her be able to participate in all school activities. She felt that next assembly she would feel braver and perhaps would require less preparation because of her success attending this assembly.

Summary of strategies

1.   Give students advance notice of the assembly.

2.   Provide details about the assembly.

3.   Let the student sit at the end of the row, and possibly near a door.

4.   Allow the student to see where he will sit during the assembly.

Points for reflection

1.   What kinds of assemblies would be difficult for students with Asperger Syndrome?

2.   How can other students help the student with Asperger Syndrome cope with attending assemblies?

School ceremonies

School ceremonies are a sign of both accomplishment and recognition. However, these ceremonies also include crowds and much noise. Sometimes the student with Asperger Syndrome can be overwhelmed by the ceremonies. Usually, some accommodations can be made so that the student with Asperger Syndrome can attend the event with minimal discomfort.

Michelle is a sixth-grade teacher who taught Robert, a student with Asperger Syndrome. Michelle knew that Robert would have trouble with graduation ceremonies at the end of sixth grade. Robert would probably begin to flap. He did this when he felt nervous. Many people, including parents, staff, and students, would be attending these ceremonies. Sometimes these ceremonies could get quite loud.

Michelle contacted the principal to ask if her class could be the first class called to the stage for students to receive their diplomas. She felt that Robert would be able to manage to come onto the stage if it was close to the beginning of the event. Then he could return to his seat or leave the event briefly, if necessary.

After she told the principal her plan, Michelle made some schedules for Robert. The first schedule showed the full day of graduation. The second schedule showed a breakdown of the events during the graduation ceremony. Michelle explained the details of these schedules and of the graduation ceremony to Robert.

Prior to the day of the graduation, Michelle brought Robert into the auditorium and showed him where he would sit. She then showed him how to walk onto the stage to receive his diploma. He practiced shaking the principal's hand, walking across the stage, and going back to his seat.

Michelle helped to build his confidence by telling Robert that he would be fine with the proceedings and that, if he felt overwhelmed or confused, he should tell her during the ceremony so that she could help him.

The graduation ceremony went smoothly. The only evidence that Robert felt anxious was when he hunched down in his seat when the piano music began. However, once he adjusted to the sound, he was able to sit upright. Robert did not need to leave the ceremony, but he said afterwards that he felt very nervous the whole time.

Summary of strategies

1. Give the student a schedule of events and explain the schedule to him.

2. Arrange for the student to go through an individual practice session if needed.

3. Allow the student to receive his award early in the ceremony in case he feels he has to leave early.

Points for reflection

1. What other accommodations might work to help a student during school ceremonies?

2. How can you make accommodations for students for ceremonies without making them stand out from other students?

Birthday parties

Often, students in elementary grades enjoy celebrating their birthdays at school. Many times, parents will send a treat or snack to school. The class will join together to sing to the student. For some students with Asperger Syndrome, the change in routine and external stimulation can make a positive experience, like the celebration of a birthday, into a difficult experience. Some students do not like others singing to them, for instance.

All students want to feel included and appreciated. However, a teacher can make small changes for a student with Asperger Syndrome so he can enjoy a birthday celebration with minimal discomfort. The accommodations that can be made for this kind of event are simple, as Janice, below, discovered.

Janice is an elementary-school teacher who teaches second grade. Janice taught a student with Asperger Syndrome named Denise. As Denise's birthday approached, Janice gave Denise a note to take home to her mother. The note indicated the type of treats Denise could bring in to share with the class to celebrate her birthday.

After Janice handed Denise the note, Denise began to get upset. She did not want to take the note home to her mother. Further, Denise told Janice that she did not want to have a birthday celebration at school because she was too nervous and that she knew it would not be fun.

Janice felt that Denise would benefit from the birthday celebration because it would help her connect with her peers. A celebration would help Denise feel like all the other students. Janice also thought that it was important that Denise try to lessen her fears so that future celebrations would not be a problem for her. She also believed that, as Denise's teacher, she needed to help Denise prepare for life.

Janice knew that Denise would enjoy a birthday party but that she needed some accommodations due to her Asperger Syndrome. To help Denise, Janice discussed with Denise in advance what would happen during the celebration. Even though the celebration would last a short amount of time, about ten minutes, Janice wanted to know Denise's thoughts about what she preferred to happen during such a celebration. Denise said that she would not mind having a party if there was no music playing and no one sang. She did not like being the center of attention.

Denise was also worried about the noise. Janice had already contacted Denise's mother who said that Denise hid under the table at an early birthday party when relatives sang to her. She became so upset that she ran upstairs to her room and would not come back out until the guests left.

Given that experience, Janice decided that the students would not sing to Denise. Instead, she decided that each of the students would reveal his or her favorite type of birthday cake to the group. In this way, Denise would have a special celebration and would not have the worry about the group singing to her.

Janice let the other students know the plan for the birthday celebration. They were very receptive to the plan and could not wait to celebrate in a different manner.

Janice took this one step further. She connected the celebration to a lesson and did a cooking unit using a cake recipe as an example. She introduced the class to reading recipes as part of measuring in mathematics class. Janice was surprised to learn how much fun the students had with all of these activities, including the birthday celebration. She realized that Denise's special needs could be a starting point for interesting lessons that can benefit the entire class.

Summary of strategies

1. Ask the student what he would like to see happen (or not happen) during his birthday celebration. Review the event ahead of time.

2. Do not force or coerce the student into participating in an event in which he would be uncomfortable.

3. Modify lessons and class activities to connect celebrations to curriculum delivery.

Points for reflection

1. For what reason might a student with Asperger Syndrome not like the song "Happy Birthday" sung to him?

2. How can you communicate the student's preferences to his classmates without making him appear unusual?

CHAPTER 2

Academic Subjects

Students with Asperger Syndrome have the normal range of intelligence. Many of these students score well on cognitive aptitude tests. Sometimes it is difficult for teachers to understand the reason that, given their intelligence, students with Asperger Syndrome have difficulty in academic areas.

For instance, students with Asperger Syndrome usually experience periods of frustration when an assignment is misunderstood. Complicated directions, sensory overload in class, or some other reason can cause the misunderstanding. These students sometimes experience meltdowns. The student may begin to cry and, at times, run out of the classroom.

The problem that the student has is not due to the difficulty of the schoolwork. The method of presentation and the anxiety over completing the task could be causing the student to feel overwhelmed. Students with Asperger Syndrome show exacerbated feelings of frustration and anxiety. Students with Asperger Syndrome have impaired sensory systems. Often, the students' emotions and senses feel magnified. The student's minor feelings of frustration can become major issues.

As an illustration, a student with Asperger Syndrome may sense the sound of a car passing on the street with the intensity of the roar of a jet engine. Similarly, frustration with a simple class assignment can turn into a traumatic event. Fortunately, there are simple and creative strategies that a teacher can use to reduce these feelings in students with Asperger Syndrome, without lowering the academic expectations for these students.

Depending on the subject, specific accommodations can be made to make schoolwork more palatable for students with Asperger Syndrome.

Although every teacher would like a perfect classroom each year, the teacher needs to accept that the "perfect classroom" is not reality. Instead, the teacher can view the challenge of making accommodations in the classroom as an opportunity to help ensure the success of all the students. Accommodations made for students with Asperger Syndrome can be effective for students with other kinds of difficulties as well.

Social studies

Social studies encompasses a multitude of subject areas, curricular materials, and teaching methods. Social studies often deals with history, the human condition, social and cultural phenomena, and current events. Since it is an abstract subject, social studies may be difficult for some students with Asperger Syndrome.

To allow the student with Asperger Syndrome to grasp the curriculum more fully, it is important that the teacher present social studies in a concrete manner. A teacher may encounter difficulty teaching social studies in a concrete manner. Traditionally teachers present these lessons in lecture format and include a tremendous number of textbook assignments. Additionally, lessons often include many related worksheets.

Students with Asperger Syndrome have impaired sensory systems, which make environmental inputs, including noises, colors, and objects, seem overwhelming. For these students, the teacher needs to structure the lesson to present information in manageable pieces or chunks.

Asha, a teacher in an elementary school, used some strategies that can make any social studies lesson more understandable and concrete. She uses the standard social studies textbook with all of her students. Kevin, a student with Asperger Syndrome, needed extra help to abbreviate the main points in the textbook. Even though he is a competent student, the substantial amount of information presented made it difficult for Kevin to narrow the amount of information to determine what was most important. Textbooks often have many illustrations, pictures, and information in the margins.

To limit the amount of information to which Kevin was exposed, Asha used brief summaries, leaving some blanks in the summaries to engage him in learning. The blanks emphasized the important items that Kevin needed to study for tests. Asha discovered that if she listed questions and sentences with blanks for completion, Kevin was able to concentrate on the material presented. Asha limited the number of pages that Kevin needed to complete (two per evening when she assigned homework). School was exhausting for Kevin. If he needed to do homework, it had to be limited.

Asha sometimes gave Kevin a small amount of homework on the weekends since he had more time to complete the work. He was able to keep up with his classmates regarding retention of information partly because of this added study opportunity.

Asha deleted extraneous information in homework assignments so that Kevin could focus on the information that he needed to know for tests. Asha knew ahead of time what would be on tests and found that making "blanks" on worksheets was simple to do. By using this technique, Asha structured the amount of textual information that Kevin had to read and remember.

When starting a new textbook chapter, Asha provided Kevin with a brief overview of the main idea of the chapter. She gave him the information on a piece of paper. She limited this overview to a few major areas. This overview helped Kevin to know when she would introduce new topics.

All of Asha's activities ensured that Kevin felt comfortable with his social studies class work and homework. Additionally, Kevin was able to use his intellect to its fullest capacity. Ultimately, he received excellent grades in this class.

It is important for teachers to understand that adapting the curriculum is not "cheating" for the student. The teacher expects the student to know the same amount of material as the other students. The accommodations described above allow a student to use his strengths in the learning process. They also help the student to overcome difficulties that arise due to having Asperger Syndrome. Many teachers find that these types of accommodations help all students learn the subject matter more deeply and decrease the drudgery associated with schoolwork.

Summary of strategies

1. Provide information summaries based on the most essential themes and topics for the student to complete.

2. Provide a brief written overview of the upcoming textbook chapter or topic.

3. Keep homework assignments brief, manageable for the student, and related to essential information.

Points for reflection

1. What other ways can you structure social studies lessons to make them seem less abstract?

2. How can making similar accommodations help all students? Can they be used with all students?

Science

Science class involves students in the scientific method, observation and description of phenomena, and theory. Science class often includes the study of concepts and events that students cannot see or feel. This may be a problem for many students with Asperger Syndrome who have difficulty with abstract concepts.

Experienced teachers use concrete examples to help explain many concepts. For example, teachers use a model of a cell or an atom when illustrating molecular structures. Science class also involves generalizing concepts to new situations, such as when the students develop theories and make discoveries. Further, science class also includes the instruction of basic facts and principles, such as the Periodic Table of the Elements.

In addition to using concrete examples to prove points, teachers use guided practice through whole class instruction, small group activities, and individual practice. The guided practice assists the students in learning to apply abstract principles to new situations. These sorts of methods are helpful to students with Asperger Syndrome. Some teachers have taken these methods a step further to ensure that learning takes place for these students.

Grace, a general science teacher from Philadelphia, teaches her students classification of different elements by asking the students to color the Periodic Table of the Elements to understand this information. Grace presents the Periodic Table on an overhead projector while students use their own paper copy at their desks. Students choose colors for the symbols for each element to identify if the substance is a solid, liquid, or gas.

Grace provides a legend at the top of the Periodic Table to guide the students as they discover the properties of each of the elements. For example, all gas symbols are colored red, all liquid symbols are colored blue, and all solids are uncolored. The resultant student product provides a visual tool for the students to conclude that most elements are solids. Grace guides the students to discover that metals, non-metals, and metalloids occur in predictable areas of the Periodic Table. She then asks the students to apply their new knowledge by giving them an element and asking what type of element it is (metal, non-metal, or a metalloid) and what phase of matter it is (solid, liquid, or gas).

Students' successes occur because of Grace's many years of teaching students and applying teaching techniques that work for students with and without disabilities. The keys to her success include making the lesson hands-on, using visuals, and using tricks with words by emphasizing a letter in the word that creates a hook to remember the definition. For example, Grace uses such a strategy for the word "theory." Write the word "thEory" with a capital "E." The "E" stands for "explanation." The definition of the word "theory" is "a possible explanation."

Grace provides typed notes and a highlighter for Logan, a student with Asperger Syndrome, so he can easily follow her lesson. She also provides the lesson for Logan on his computer so he can make changes to the document to suit his learning needs. Logan also uses his laptop during labs in science class not only to follow the systematic procedures for the lab, but also to record the data he collects. Grace has created the necessary tables and charts for Logan to input his data into the computer.

The purpose of lab experiments is to collect and analyze data, and not to test Logan on his ability to organize the data. Grace chooses a cooperative partner to work with Logan for lab experiments. When using dangerous chemicals or fire in the lab, Grace provides direct observation to ensure safety rules are followed.

Another teacher, Pete, wondered how he could help his student, Loni, to feel less fearful when doing lab experiments. Loni is a student who has Asperger Syndrome. She is very intelligent, but was very nervous around the instruments and equipment in the lab. Pete tried to find out why Loni was fearful. He asked her many questions and concluded that Loni was simply uncomfortable with the unpredictability of the lab experiments. Loni did not know the outcome of many of the experiments. Her feelings made it impossible for her to participate fully in the lab experience. Pete decided he would need to eliminate the aspect of uncertainty in the lab outcomes for Loni to be comfortable in completing experiments.

First, he chose a competent, compassionate student to be Loni's lab partner. He thought about ways to minimize Loni's anxiety. About one week prior to the lab (the class had one lab period per week), Pete gave Loni a paper with a brief description of the lab. This way she would know well in advance the lab topic. The next day he gave Loni a simple list of procedures to be followed for the lab. He included in this list Loni's activities that she needed to complete. By doing this, Loni became very familiar with lab procedures and knew exactly what was expected of her.

Loni was given an opportunity to ask Pete questions in advance of the lab if she needed clarification. Some of the students had complained that Loni was slow in following the directions in her part of the lab, and this procedure also helped increase Loni's speed. One day prior to the lab, Pete gave Loni another worksheet that explained the outcome of the lab. He gave the facts of the lab and the result. Loni took the worksheet home and looked over it the night before the lab.

This procedure helped Loni in many ways. It helped her become an efficient lab partner because she understood the lab procedures and outcomes. Loni found that her anxiety decreased during the lab. Her lab grade increased because she was able to make better connections between the lab work and class work, as she could focus better on the lab theories. Additionally, her confidence increased each time she performed a new lab experiment successfully.

Summary of strategies

1. Color-code materials to make abstract concepts more concrete.

2. Provide a paper copy of class notes prior to the class.

3. Provide numerous opportunities to practice in various settings.

4. Allow the use of the computer for note-taking revisions and additions.

5. Allow the use of the computer for data collection.

6. Provide the student with lab procedures prior to the lab class, so the student can review them and ask questions beforehand if needed.

Points for reflection

1. What other methods might help a student to understand abstract science concepts?

2. What accommodations might you want to consider regarding safety during lab experiments for students with Asperger Syndrome?

Mathematics (general)

Mathematics is the use of numbers to manipulate, calculate, and quantify real-life situations. Mathematics evolved over time due to the need to solve everyday problems that required quantifying and comparing information. The teaching of mathematics in schools has shifted from having students learn by rote and memorization of facts to investigative learning. In investigative learning, teachers give students a problem without a method for solving it.

Mathematics is an area in which many students with Asperger Syndrome have difficulty. In many schools, teachers use a mathematics program that is based upon abstract concepts and uses investigative, inquiry-based learning. However, students with Asperger Syndrome usually need help understanding this approach because it requires a great deal of abstract thinking. Students with Asperger Syndrome and other disabilities that affect learning need repetition and consistency to be able to learn basic math concepts. Students with Asperger Syndrome can then learn advanced concepts using the same techniques. However, if the teachers make adaptations to the teaching method, these students may find investigative, inquiry-based learning interesting and enjoyable.

Ron, a seventh-grade mathematics teacher, found that Mandeep, a student with Asperger Syndrome, became quite upset whenever Ron introduced new concepts. Ron knew that Mandeep was quite intelligent and could think logically.

Ron wanted to find a method of teaching Mandeep mathematics so that he could learn new concepts with a minimum of frustration. He knew that Mandeep got frustrated very easily. One day, rather than orally introducing a new topic, Ron wrote a new mathematics problem on the board with a question mark beside it. He did this before his students entered the classroom. As they entered, Ron stated nothing about the problem. Mandeep was intrigued and asked how to solve the problem.

Other students in his classroom became equally interested. Subsequently, Ron began all of his lessons in this manner. This simple approach removed much of the anxiety regarding the presentation of new mathematics lessons for many of his students.

Brenda, a fourth-grade mathematics teacher, had Jacob, a student with Asperger Syndrome, in her class. Several weeks into the school year, Brenda gave her students daily one-page mathematics homework assignments. Jacob did not turn in any of his mathematics assignments. Jacob's mother called Brenda and stated that Jacob could not do the work at home. Jacob's mother also said that when she approached Jacob about doing the work, he began to cry and flap. His mother concluded that Jacob was overwhelmed by how the homework looked on the page.

Brenda decided that she would change the format of Jacob's mathematics assignments. She revised the worksheets to include fewer problems per page. She designed the page so that there was much more "white space." She also placed the problems farther apart on the page. Brenda also decreased the number of problems from 20 to 10 per night. Jacob's mom reported that this accommodation helped relieve much of

Jacob's anxiety so that he was able to complete most of the homework problems each evening.

Another option for teaching mathematics to the student with Asperger Syndrome begins with the teacher closely examining the current mathematics curriculum. Some mathematics curricula are more concrete and others are more abstract. If simple changes do not result in success for a student who has Asperger Syndrome, the teacher may want to consider changing curricular materials. Some students need a mathematics program that is less inquiry based and more concrete. That is, the teacher gives the students a method for problem solving and students are simply required to follow such steps. Such a program typically involves a great deal of drill and practice. School personnel can choose from several mathematics programs that are more concrete and can be more accessible for many students with Asperger Syndrome. These programs have been useful to teach math to students with other difficulties as well.

Noah, a fifth-grade teacher, noticed that his student who has Asperger Syndrome, Marcus, was doing extremely poorly in math. Marcus had high grades in all other subject areas. Noah realized that the way he was presenting mathematics in the classroom was not working for Marcus. Noah also noticed that a couple of other students in his classroom were also not performing well in mathematics. Noah discussed the situation with Marcus' special education teacher. The special education teacher was interested in an alternative approach to teaching mathematics to Marcus and a small number of other students in Noah's classroom who were having difficulties.

This teacher came into Noah's classroom and taught mathematics to this small group of students. All the students in the group responded well to the new mathematics curriculum. Noah realized that this mathematics situation was another example of how students learn the same concepts in different ways and that a teacher could help a student with Asperger Syndrome learn by using some creative strategies.

Summary of strategies

1. Use specially prepared worksheets to limit the amount of problems on a page to make mathematics homework less intimidating.

2. Try a concrete-type approach to teaching mathematics, as opposed to inquiry-based, investigative learning.

3. Use non-verbal information, such as visual cues, illustrations, and photographs.

4. Pursue alternative curricular materials that use repetition and consistency to reinforce basic concepts.

Points for reflection

1. What are other ways to reduce feelings of frustration in mathematics instruction without lowering expectations of students?

2. Why would non-verbal forms of instructional input be beneficial to students with Asperger Syndrome?

Mathematics (word problems)

Aside from basic facts, mathematics is the use of numbers to manipulate, calculate, and quantify real-life situations. Part of the mathematics curriculum involves students in solving word problems, which can reflect problems that crop up in everyday life.

Carlo is a fifth-grade student with Asperger Syndrome. Carlo's teacher, Nancy, met with Carlo's family so she could prepare for his arrival in her classroom for the new school year. Nancy discovered that Carlo enjoys tactile activities. She felt that he would respond well to hands-on activities to learn the information presented in fifth grade. Nancy teaches the students to solve word problems that require the students to find a fractional part of a whole. Nancy, through peer collaboration, has developed a hands-on approach to solving these types of word problems. By leading the students in the process of solving word problems, Nancy teaches the students how to gather and assess information. This information assessment is critical to solving word problems successfully. Since this information assessment is abstract, Nancy believed that she needed to make changes to standard curricular materials to teach Carlo how to solve word problems.

Prior to teaching the students how to find the fractional part of a whole, Nancy reviewed the definitions of the terms "numerator" and "denominator" with the students. To show this in a concrete manner, Nancy drew rectangles on the board. She then asked the students to go to the board and shade fractional parts of a rectangle. The students demonstrated many concepts, including the following: "Shade two-fifths of the rectangle." As the student drew the rectangle and divided it into five pieces, Nancy asked, "Why was the rectangle divided into five equal pieces?" After the students shaded in two of the five pieces, Nancy asked, "Why were only two pieces shaded?" After all the students had a chance to demonstrate their knowledge on the board, Nancy felt comfortable that the students understood the meaning of "numerator" and "denominator."

Using the overhead projector, Nancy then showed the question "You purchased a 15-pound bag of dog food and have fed the dog one-third of the bag. How many pounds of dog food did you feed the dog?" She told the students to use the square tiles in their mathematics toolbox to solve the problem.

Carlo understood this definite and concrete instruction. He counted 15 tiles to represent the 15 pounds of dog food. Remembering the concept reviewed earlier in the class period, Carlo decided to divide the tiles into three equal piles since the denominator was three. He realized that since the numerator was one, he needed to use only one of the piles. Finally, he concluded that the dog ate five pounds of dog food since there were five tiles in each group. After Nancy demonstrated the solution to the problem, Carlo was excited that he had solved the problem correctly.

Nancy distributed similar problems for the students to solve with their assigned mathematics partner. Nancy permitted the students to use the mathematics tiles and any other materials from their mathematics toolbox. After practicing several problems using these items, Nancy asked the students to put away their mathematics toolboxes. She instructed the class to take out their whiteboards. Nancy showed the class how to use dots or "X"s to solve the fractional part of the whole problems. The students understood the concept of using only paper and pencil to determine the answers. Since Carlo was successful with the majority of the problems, he felt confident that he would be able to complete the problems that Nancy assigned for homework.

Nancy found that teaching a new concept by explaining it at a concrete level allows all of her students, including a student with Asperger Syndrome, to understand the concepts of problem solving. Although many teachers may feel that teaching in a concrete manner is time consuming, Nancy feels the time invested in this discovery process is worthwhile. The students retain the idea that they can solve many problems at the concrete level. Additionally, this method of teaching is accessible to the student with Asperger Syndrome.

Nancy posts her practice problems, procedures to solve the problems, and solutions on the school's website. She does this to allow students and parents to obtain extra assistance and information. Carlo's parents also email Nancy in the evening to let her know if he had difficulties understanding and completing the homework. If Carlo had difficulties with the homework, Nancy follows up with him in the morning to re-teach the concepts to him. This way he can continue to review and master mathematical concepts without creating gaps in his mathematical knowledge. Carlo's family and Nancy have discovered that this technique has been successful in reducing his anxiety in the school setting.

With these accommodations, Carlo does not feel like he is constantly behind the rest of the class, and he is more attentive to the class discussion because he understands the previous concepts. In mathematics, it is important that the students have a continuous pattern of learning without gaps. If not, the students may feel lost when new concepts are presented.

Summary of strategies

1. Allow students to explore problem solving independently by asking guiding questions.

2.   Students need to investigate and discover solutions to problems with hands-on materials.

3.   Provide students with guided notes, additional problems, and time for the re-teaching of concepts.

4.   Structure the lessons to use concrete methods of problem solving.

5.   Have students use hands-on materials, and gradually transition to more abstract methods of problem solving.

6.   Allow the students to work with a partner so they can discuss methods for solving a problem.

7.   Give homework that reinforces the method of problem solving provided in class.

Points for reflection

1.   Given the demands of the curriculum, how would you suggest that you balance the time it takes for students to do hands-on problem solving versus direct instruction?

2.   How would communication with parents help a student with Asperger Syndrome experience less frustration in learning mathematics?

Geometry

Zia, a middle-school mathematics instructor, teaches geometry. Zia allows the students to use hands-on materials and guided notes to enable them to be successful. Dean is a seventh-grade student with Asperger Syndrome in Zia's class. Dean has a solid foundation of mathematical skills, but struggles with abstract concepts. Zia has known Dean since he was in fifth grade because the mathematics team at Zia's school works with the fifth- and sixth-graders for two periods in a six-day cycle. Due to these prior interactions, Zia and Dean have a comfortable student–teacher relationship. Since Zia knows Dean fairly well, he is able to detect when Dean becomes anxious during a mathematics lesson.

When Dean becomes excited or uneasy he bounces his legs. Zia knows that Dean's behavior is a sign that he needs to change his teaching strategy to refocus Dean on the lesson he is presenting.

Zia discovered that Dean had a difficult time remembering the formula for the volume of a square pyramid. Formulas are an abstract idea, and students often do not understand how they relate to the real world. Zia decided to involve all students in a hands-on experiment to enable the students to discover the formula.

By using this discovery technique, Zia felt that Dean would understand the basis for the formula because he could see how the formula actually works. Zia thought that the students should work in partners so each student could be involved in the discovery of the formula.

Zia gave the students a rectangular prism and a pyramid with the same base and height measurements. Zia also gave the students a cup and a bucket of play sand. Zia explained the experiment verbally after he distributed the written directions. Zia directed the students to find a relationship between the volume of the prism and that of the pyramid. Although Dean was confused, his partner began to fill one of the objects with sand. Zia mingled with the students and provided some guidance to help them discover a relationship that involves the volume of the two objects.

Dean and his partner realized that the volume of the pyramid was less than the volume of the prism. They decided to find how many pyramids it would take to make one prism by filling the pyramid with sand and dumping the contents of the pyramid into the prism. They continued this process until the prism was full. Dean and his partner discovered that three pyramids of sand filled one prism.

After the students were finished with the experiments, they discussed the results in a group. Zia requested that Dean and his partner demonstrate the procedures used to develop the correct formula for the group. Dean showed some signs of anxiety, but agreed to participate by filling the rectangular pyramid and transferring the sand to the rectangular prism while his partner explained the process.

Summary of strategies

1. The use of guided notes allows the student with Asperger Syndrome to focus on the important information that is being taught.

2. Assign an appropriate partner for the student with Asperger Syndrome.

3. If the student with Asperger Syndrome is capable, request that he demonstrate procedures for the class with a partner.

Points for reflection

1. How can the lesson be taught concretely?

2. Can the student with Asperger Syndrome work with a pre-assigned peer to facilitate learning the lesson?

3. How can the students discover the concept of the lesson without being told every step of the process?

Language arts

Reading

Reading may or may not be difficult for students with Asperger Syndrome. This section does not focus on how to teach a student with Asperger Syndrome who has a reading disability how to read. Instead, this section gives ideas about how to make the student with Asperger Syndrome who is already reading enjoy reading more fully and lessen anxiety that the student may feel in the reading class.

The choice of books that a teacher assigns for the reading class can have a definite impact on the success of the student with Asperger Syndrome. Students with Asperger Syndrome may have fears and aversions to things in everyday life that other people do not consider. For example, many students with Asperger Syndrome are afraid of dogs or bees. These creatures are often unpredictable and can be dangerous.

If the teacher knows that the student has these fears, she should keep this in mind when she is choosing a book for the class to read. She would not want to reinforce the fear that the student with Asperger Syndrome already experiences. Additionally, if the student reads a particular book that contains a scene that disturbs him, he may not want to read anything further. Therefore, the teacher should determine the student's particular sensitivities and avoid books that could exacerbate them.

In the same way, a teacher's choice of books can help a student with Asperger Syndrome learn far more than merely how to read the content of the book. Many books can help teach the student social skills without direct instruction. Many books involve relationships between people, and the portrayal of appropriate relationships and interactions between people can help the student with Asperger Syndrome to learn social skills.

The more ways that the student is exposed to positive interactions, the more likely he is to imitate appropriate social skills. By choosing reading material with this in mind, the reading teacher can provide an indirect support for the student with Asperger Syndrome.

Another idea which the reading teacher can consider when choosing a book for the students to read is the special interest of the student with Asperger Syndrome. Often, the student with Asperger Syndrome can be inspired to read and learn by the teacher assigning the class a book that directly interests that student. Mandy, a sixth-grade teacher, found this to be the case.

Mandy teaches reading to sixth-graders. She had a student in her class named Hassan, who has Asperger Syndrome. Mandy knew that Hassan had certain fears of loud noises and flashing lights. Since she wanted to engage Hassan with the entire class, Mandy kept him in mind when she was determining the reading list for the year. Mandy did not choose any books that had topics that could be frightening to Hassan, such as thunder or earthquakes.

Mandy knew that Hassan had a special fondness for wheels, automobiles, and things that spun around. She decided to choose a book for the students to read that was a novel where the main character was a teenager who was interested in racecar driving. She felt that the entire class would be interested in the story, and that the topic would especially interest Hassan.

Since Hassan tended to flap or rock during class discussions, Mandy wanted to find a way for him to participate with the class. After assigning the first chapter of the book to the class, Mandy asked the class their feelings about the book. Hassan immediately raised his hand and said that he loved reading about the automobiles and the dream of the teenager to be a racecar driver. Although some of the students did not like the topic, Mandy felt that she had finally found a way to engage Hassan in the classroom discussion.

Mandy decided that the next book would deal with some adolescent issues between girls and boys. She chose a particular book because there was much dialogue between people, and it dealt with peer pressure issues. During the discussion of the book, Mandy tried to bring out the social issues involved that went beyond the mere content of the book.

The class had several days of discussions regarding peer pressure and even role-played some of the scenes from the book. Since Hassan was comfortable with class, he enjoyed participating in the discussion. It was interesting for Hassan's peers to hear his thoughts about topics, and Mandy was convinced that her choice of reading material directly contributed to Hassan's participation in the class.

Aside from keeping Hassan in mind while choosing the books for the class to read, Mandy also found that Hassan and all her students benefited from a brief summary of the book given to them prior to reading the book itself. By having the summary, Hassan felt less anxiety reading the book, because he knew it did not revolve around any situations that he feared.

Summary of strategies

1.   Choose books that do not involve topics that will disturb the sensitivities of the student with Asperger Syndrome.

2.   Investigate books outside the usual curriculum that focus on the student's special interest to involve the student in both reading and class discussion.

3.   Choose books that deal with social interactions and relationships to help the student with Asperger Syndrome to learn these skills indirectly.

4. Briefly summarize the book for the class so the student with Asperger Syndrome will feel comfortable that the book does not include topics about which he is highly sensitive.

Points for reflection

1. As a reading teacher, do you feel comfortable going outside the curriculum to choose books for reading? Is this something that can be done at your school?

2. Remember how books that you have read affected your emotions and relationships. Do you understand how the choice of books can directly affect both the students' learning and the atmosphere in the classroom?

3. Consider why it is important for the student with Asperger Syndrome to participate in discussions with the whole class.

Writing

Students with Asperger Syndrome may have problems with gross and fine motor activities. Many students with this syndrome have poor muscle tone in general. These physical weaknesses can make it challenging for the student to learn to hold and use a pencil. The student's handwriting may also be difficult to decipher because of poorly formed letters. Additionally, students with Asperger Syndrome may not have the stamina for long writing assignments. Even if they have good ideas, getting the ideas out of their head and onto the page can be a challenge.

Although it may not be apparent, the writing difficulty also makes it harder for these students to take tests. Therefore, teachers may not correctly assess the student's knowledge of a subject area (see "General testing" on p. 84 for more information). As you can imagine, these issues relating to writing follow these students throughout their school careers. This problem can become worse as each year passes.

There are two parts of the writing process in which students with Asperger Syndrome need assistance. The first part involves helping the student grip the pencil. Teachers can then work with students on learning and practicing writing the letters of the alphabet.

On many tests and assessments, poor legibility has a negative effect on grades. The teachers should assess the content of answers in order to determine if the student mastered the material presented. The neatness of the paper does not reflect the cognitive ability of the students. Teachers seem to feel that if a paper is messy, then the student did not care or did not make appropriate effort to complete the assignment.

In the earlier grades, teachers focus on teaching penmanship. Students with Asperger Syndrome learn at this time that they do not measure up to their peers in this regard. It is important for the self-esteem of these students that teachers make simple accommodations in the early grades. Initially, accommodations include allowing the student to form letters and practice at his own pace.

James is a second-grade teacher who encourages creative writing and the expression of ideas. Stephan is a student with Asperger Syndrome. Stephan frequently became upset when he received the daily journal writing assignment. This journal assignment consists of drawing a picture and writing a sentence. James noticed that Stephan could draw a picture and tell about his drawing, but he did not want to write a sentence describing the picture.

James first gave Stephan a pencil that had a larger diameter, a "fat" pencil, so that Stephan could grip the pencil more easily. Another option that James had considered was to give Stephan a triangular grip to fit on the pencil and make it easier to hold. Stephan had already tried this "triangle grip" in first grade and did not like the feeling of this grip, so James did not make him try the grip again.

After James changed the type of pencil that was used, he also modified the assignment for Stephan. James told Stephan that he only had to write one word, the first word of his sentence, after he drew the picture. James asked the classroom aide to write the rest of the sentence for Stephan after he dictated it to her. After two weeks of only writing one word, James increased the requirement to two words per sentence. By breaking down the assignment into shorter segments, Stephan practiced his writing and gradually he was able to build his stamina to be able to write more words.

James made a point of praising Stephan with each extra word that he wrote, so that Stephan knew James noticed his extra effort. Over the year, James gave Stephan the option of using more words until he was comfortable writing a sentence. This low-pressure approach resulted in Stephan feeling calmer during journal writing. Stephan also learned to write letters carefully and slowly so the words were legible to the reader. James wanted to teach Stephan that he should be more concerned about the quality of his letters and words than the quantity of what he had written. James believed that, if he taught Stephan to form and choose his letters and words carefully, Stephan would be more successful when writing in the higher levels of school.

For other longer writing assignments, such as a short story about what the students did over winter break, James required some writing from Stephan, but less than for other students. For instance, Stephan is required to write the title, his name, and related information. The rest of the essay is scribed by the classroom aide, or typed on a keyboard. James also allows Stephan's parents to scribe some homework, whether it is sentences for spelling words or short paragraphs.

Nicholas is a student in Ken's fourth-grade class. As part of their social studies assignment, the students are required to do some research at the library and online. They have to write their findings on index cards and then present the information verbally to the class. Nicholas felt overwhelmed by the entire assignment.

Nicholas could not follow the directions and had no idea about how to use the library for research. He knew how to use the Internet, but could not figure out how to do any research on his topic. After speaking to him about the entire assignment, Ken realized what was bothering Nicholas. Nicholas could not understand how he would manage to fit all the information about his subject on the small index cards.

Ken had decided to have the students to use these cards since he felt that by using the cards the students would learn how to keep the research concise. He felt that the index cards were a good way to keep the information organized and succinct. However, these cards were new to the students. For Nicholas, who has Asperger Syndrome, the new cards, combined with the directions for completing the assignment, were over-whelming. Nicholas could not focus on the task required because he was too "flipped out" by having to use the index cards instead of his regular paper. It seemed "too hard" for him and he gave up. He did not believe that he could even begin the research. Ken did not think that the index cards would present a problem for anyone. Most of the students felt excited with the idea of taking notes in a different way. Nicholas did not think this change was fun or exciting.

Once Ken realized the problem, he told Nicholas that he could continue to take notes on regular notebook paper. Ken also suggested that Nicholas might want to take notes on the computer or have someone write the notes for him. He assured Nicholas that the idea of the assign-ment was to learn to do research. Nicholas did not have to worry about the method that he chose to write the notes.

Nicholas was extremely relieved. He could not make the connection, without help, that his issue with the index cards was not such a challenge. Given his concrete thinking, he wanted to follow every direction and then became anxious and flustered when he encountered a problem. Ken could not believe how easy it was to solve Nicholas' dilemma. He was glad he listened to Nicholas to find out exactly what was bothering him, because Ken never would have guessed the cause of Nicholas' anxiety.

The other aspect of writing that students encounter occurs in the higher grades, such as fifth grade and above. In these grades, students are often required to focus on one particular topic and write paragraphs about specific current events or history subjects, or to answer a lengthy science question. It is hoped that the student with Asperger Syndrome has managed to compensate for his fine motor skill deficits in school, or teachers have made accommodations to help the student in this area. Often, these students use a keyboard or a scribe for lengthy writing assignments.

The student with Asperger Syndrome usually has an extremely narrow area of interest and has a hard time transferring his attention onto some other topic. If the student needs to write about a specific science or social studies topic, then he will have to focus on that topic in order to get the assignment finished. The student with Asperger Syndrome may be unable to focus on a topic long enough to finish a writing assignment.

Teachers will need to make accommodations to the curriculum to allow the student with Asperger Syndrome to write about his particular areas of interest.

Edward was a sixth-grade English teacher who liked to have his students read books and write book recommendations. Book recommendations are a summary of the book and discuss whether the student liked the book enough to recommend it to others. Angelo, a student with Asperger Syndrome, liked to read Nintendo Power magazines because he was very interested in video games, the history of video games, and the designers of video games.

Angelo's mother reported that he read for over an hour when he came home from school; however, he only read the magazines, and not many books. Edward decided that he would allow Angelo to do "book recommendations" on different video-gaming magazine articles. Instead of choosing a book to review, Angelo chose three articles and reported on them. Angelo loved to write about these topics and the class learned interesting information from his presentations. Edward felt that the accommodation benefited both Angelo and the entire class. The students in the class also began to recognize Angelo as an expert in video games, which helped him to socialize better with his peers.

Summary of strategies

1. Provide students with a special writing pencil or special grip if necessary.

2. Shorten the writing assignment for the student.

3. Allow the student to use a computer to write lengthy assignments.

4. Allow the student to choose the topic he wishes to write about, if possible.

5. Provide a scribe for the student to allow him to verbalize his ideas without the pressure of actually having to write.

Points for reflection

1.   What do you feel is the most important aspect of teaching the student to write?

2.   What ways could you encourage a student to write creatively if he struggles with penmanship issues (and therefore does not enjoy writing)?

Literature

Students with Asperger Syndrome sometimes discover that reading and understanding non-fiction work is difficult. Students with Asperger Syndrome view their world in concrete terms. Literature exposes students to writings that consist of creative thoughts that the student can interpret in various ways.

Sue, a fourth-grade teacher, has her students perform a readers' theater unit. Sam is a student with Asperger Syndrome in Sue's class who has a difficult time writing stories. As is typical for students with Asperger Syndrome, Sam has some specific areas of interest. Sue discovered that although Sam struggles to complete writing assignments, he does much better with writing if Sue bases the assignment around an area of his interest. If the subject does not interest Sam at all, he will usually be unable to complete the writing activities.

This semester Sue has chosen the play *The Crazy Critters* (Walker 2001) for the topic of her readers' theater groups. Sue offered this script to Sam's group. She believed Sam would enjoy this story. Sam and a few of his peers in the group are fascinated with animals. The roles for the script were chosen by Sue and assigned to the students.

The students brought props for the script to school. The group practiced their play, with their costumes and props, in an assigned area of the room. Sue made sure that Sam had a mask to wear as part of his costume. Sam was leery of practicing the play, but he felt less exposed if he wore a mask. He said that he felt as if "I'm not the one practicing. He is just my character." Each of the groups practiced the play for about ten minutes each day. The groups then performed their plays for each other at the end of the unit.

Sue arranged for the students to perform the play in the classroom, as opposed to the auditorium. Therefore, Sam did not have to worry about a change of environment. Although Sam was slightly nervous, he was comfortable with the audience of his peers and the classroom environment.

Chris, a middle-school teacher, asked her students to read *King Arthur and the Knights of the Round Table* (Pyle *et al.* 2002). She then distributed the final writing project for the book. Chris' student Namid has Asperger Syndrome and has a difficult time writing about the stories that have been read and discussed in class. However, Namid enjoys talking about the adventures of medieval knights and playing video games with a medieval theme.

In order to make the writing assignment more hands-on, Chris packed boxes of different items from medieval times. She instructed the students to choose one box and to write an adventure story that included the items contained in the box. The box that fascinated Namid contained replicas of a Celtic cross, castle, knight's helmet, knight's shield, a picture of a suit of armor, a medieval knight snow globe, a rock, a picture of King Arthur's dagger, an antique purse watch, a rock waterfall fountain, a family crest, a dragon, and a mandarin ivory tusk.

Chris provided the students with a worksheet clearly showing the adventure story. She also had handouts listing each of the items in the boxes, so the students would remember the items while they were working at home. Namid was relieved that he only needed to incorporate six items from the box into his story. The students spent a class period looking at the items and writing a rough draft of the story. Chris instructed the students to complete the final draft of the story at home with parents' assistance. Namid was glad that he would be able to complete the story at home.

Summary of strategies

1.   Since students with Asperger Syndrome tend to view the world in black-and-white terms, some types of literature may be difficult for these students to comprehend. This may be particularly true if the literature is not based in reality, such as is the case with science fiction.

2.   Remember to use the students' strengths, such as their special interests, when planning projects.

3.   Students with Asperger Syndrome may be able to act in plays more willingly if they have costume to "hide" them.

4.   Allow students to complete writing assignments at home with the parents' assistance.

Points for reflection

1.   Will the planned project place unnecessary stress on the student with Asperger Syndrome?

2.   Have you researched the needs of the student with Asperger Syndrome in relation to the content of project?

3.   How can you make a difficult writing task less intimidating for the student with Asperger Syndrome?

Health

Health class covers many different topics as the student progresses through the grades. Topics such as good dental hygiene, bones of the human body, the process of digestion, the effects of drugs and alcohol on the body, puberty, reproduction, and death and dying are taught to students in various grade levels. Most of these topics cover basic information; however, the difficulty for students with Asperger Syndrome is the way that these students process the presented information.

The student with Asperger Syndrome interprets the health information very literally. These students tend to learn rules and follow these rules precisely. The student with Asperger Syndrome interprets the rule

"No alcohol" to mean "No alcohol ever, no matter what the circum-stance." Some cough syrups contain a small degree of alcohol.

To the student with Asperger Syndrome, this rule becomes a basic rule to follow and one that the student will enforce on others as he becomes older. For this reason, the teacher must carefully consider the content of any rules that she teaches to the student.

Taylor, a fifth-grade student with Asperger Syndrome, was learning about drugs through the anti-drug-use program entitled "D.A.R.E." (D.A.R.E. America 1996). The local law enforcement officer presented the program to the students. Throughout the school year, students would be involved in related anti-drug activities that were part of the program. Taylor seemed to like participating in these activities. It was a surprise to the staff of the middle school when Taylor refused to participate in the formal graduation ceremony of the D.A.R.E. program.

The ceremony consisted of the students going onto the stage to receive a diploma and talking about what they learned in the program. Since the staff did not anticipate any difficulties with the graduation program, Taylor did not practice and was not prepared to participate in the routine graduation. Based on Taylor's refusal to attend graduation, his teacher created scripts and practiced similar events with him to prepare him for future events (see section entitled "Assemblies" on p. 47).

Scripts describe situations in a written story format. Teachers and other school staff often present students with Autism Spectrum Disorders with scripts to prepare them for upcoming events and to teach social skills. Carol Gray (2000) developed a program for creating "Social Stories[TM]."

Since the time when Chase, a student with Asperger Syndrome, was very young, his parents, Alex and Megan, were honest with him. In their house, Chase's parents taught Chase and his siblings anatomically correct vocabulary. Chase's parents provided their children with facts about reproduction and the cycle of life.

His parents did not expect Chase to become upset when his fifth-grade teacher announced that the class was going to learn about puberty. They previewed the video that the teacher would show to the class. Chase's parents did not think that any information in the video would disturb him. However, Chase was uncomfortable discussing such "private" topics in a classroom. Chase also thought that he knew this information and did not understand why he needed to learn it again. The teacher agreed to pre-test Chase on puberty information. Since he did well on this test, the teacher permitted Chase to go to the library to read while other students watched the video and discussed puberty topics.

As Chase became older, his peers often responded with teasing when he used anatomically accurate terminology. He did not understand why some students were cruel and teased him. A teacher overheard several students bullying Chase. The teacher referred Chase to the guidance counselor to ascertain what the students were saying to Chase. The students who bullied Chase admitted to doing so. They taunted him because he used vocabulary that was not common in school. Chase's guidance counselor worked with Chase to teach him words that his peers commonly use. The counselor and principal worked with Chase's peers to stop them from bullying him.

Mattie is the eleventh-grade health teacher for Curt, a student with Asperger Syndrome. Each year Mattie teaches a unit on death and dying. The unit culminates with the class touring a casket- (coffin) making company. The class also visits a funeral home to learn about the job duties of a mortician. Students and their parents have the option of attending these fieldtrips or completing an alternative assignment.

Mattie communicated with Curt's parents throughout the entire semester to be sure that she was sensitive to Curt's needs in the classroom. She made a variety of changes to the lesson to accommodate for Curt's learning style. Curt's parents reviewed with him what would happen on the fieldtrip and agreed that he should go. After the fieldtrip, Curt and his parents discussed the process that occurs after a person dies. Curt summarized the fieldtrip by making a piece of artwork that expressed his emotions of peace and serenity about the death of his grandparent. Curt's parents were pleased with the unit Mattie taught.

Summary of strategies

1.   Teach common language usage.

2.   Keep teaching of the facts simple and honest.

3.   Remember to review procedures regarding assemblies or other ceremonies.

> ## Points for reflection
>
> 1.   Is a student with Asperger Syndrome in your school teased about the vocabulary he uses?
>
> 2.   How can the teacher integrate fieldtrips into the curriculum to enhance the learning process of real-life situations for students with Asperger Syndrome?
>
> 3.   Is the student able to express his knowledge through alternative assessments?

Geography

Sharon, a seventh-grade geography teacher, has learned through experience that students learn best when they complete hands-on activities. Sharon's student with Asperger Syndrome, Amy, prefers to work independently or with only one partner in geography class. In order to teach her students about the various types of maps, Sharon introduces her students to an activity entitled *Orange World* (Lewandowski 2000).

This activity incorporates the senses of smelling, tasting, touching, and seeing by using an orange as a representation of the world. Sharon explained the activity to Amy's class. Since Amy has excellent drawing skills, she took the lead and began to draw the continents and major grid lines such as the Equator, Prime Meridian, and the Tropics of Capricorn and Cancer onto the orange with a permanent marker. Amy's partner assisted her by labeling each continent and line after it was drawn. Using the school's digital camera, Amy took a picture of their orange after it was drawn and labeled.

The next day in class, Amy and her partner made an incision around the Equator and carefully lifted the two hemispheres off the fruit by using a spoon. Amy and her partner then followed the directions and created two projection-type maps with the orange. Amy was asked to make a controlled projection and her partner was asked to use the "smashing" technique. Amy carefully tried to lay her hemisphere flat on the desktop by doing her best to control where the breaks of the orange occurred. Amy was attempting to create a controlled projection. Her partner had the task of smashing her hemisphere flat, creating an uncontrolled projection. Amy was glad that her partner agreed to be the person to smash the orange. Amy knew that she would not be able to tolerate the feeling of smashing the orange. The partner then took more digital pictures of their new orange halves.

Amy and her partner talked about what they learned about perspective from performing the map activity. Amy's partner did the writing for the activity because Amy had difficulty writing. The students learned through the hands-on experience about the various types of map projections and their general characteristics. Amy enjoyed this assignment not only because she was able to contribute to the partnership by being the main artist, but also because she learned about the geography of land and water masses of the earth. Sharon finds that this activity is an effective teaching tool since it incorporates many of the senses. She was pleased that Amy, despite her difficulties, was able to participate fully in the activity. Additionally, students work with partners, which enables each student to use his strengths to contribute to the completion of the project.

Gary, a geography teacher, instructs his students on the geography of France and Paris, including discussing the importance of major landmarks in Paris. This year Gary has decided to teach the lesson a little bit differently to accommodate the needs of Casey, a student with Asperger Syndrome. He showed his students a video entitled *City Life in Europe* (Discovery Communications, Inc. 2004), and required them to take notes on the video. Gary provided a guided note page for Casey to complete which included major landmarks, neighboring countries, and bodies of water. The class used classroom resources and the Internet to complete geographical maps of France and research important landmarks of the country. Gary provided Casey with study guides to assist him in locating essential information on the project. Gary asked the students to create two scrapbook pages after studying three famous landmarks in France. He gave the students a grading rubric that detailed all of the important information that the students needed to include on the scrapbook pages. Casey used class time to research the project. Each student met with Gary individually during breaks to review their progress with him. The students' final projects were displayed in the classroom. Casey and his family were proud of the work that Casey did to complete his scrapbook pages. Due to the nature of the project, Casey's family was able to assist him with it to reduce his level of stress.

Samir discovered a method to help his student with Asperger Syndrome, Philip, learn the location of different countries on a map. Samir was teaching the students about the continent of South America. Most students, including Philip, did not know anything about the location, climate, or culture of the countries in South America. Usually, Samir begins his lesson about a new continent with the students learning the location of the countries within the continent.

However, Philip got very upset and began to flap when Samir gave out the map of South America and Samir explained the assignment. Samir instructed the students to learn all the countries and to study for a test scheduled at the end of week. Philip simply flapped and looked out the window. As Philip was walking out of the classroom door he muttered, "You might as well flunk me. I'll never learn that."

Samir knew that he was referring to the map of South America, and gave some thought as to how he could help Philip learn the map with a minimum of stress. Samir thought that if he could break the map into smaller sections, Philip would be able to learn the countries. Samir made three maps for Philip to memorize. Each map showed several countries from the continent of South America. First, Samir gave Philip the maps that had the countries labeled. After Philip learned the countries, Samir gave Philip maps that were unlabeled, but contained a word bank of the countries contained on the map. By limiting the amount of information that Philip had to learn, Samir made learning countries much less stressful for Philip.

Summary of strategies

1.   Create projects that are hands-on and multi-sensory to help students to capitalize on their academic strengths.

2.   Incorporate and encourage technology into student projects.

Points for reflection

1.   What projects can you create for the student to experience success in your classroom?

2.   How can you create study guides to assist students in taking notes?

3.   Can you distribute a rubric to provide students with a road map for success?

4.   Will you allow a student's family to assist in completing class projects?

History

History, the study of past events, is a subject taught in schools around the world. Students study written accounts of events in order to help them understand people and the relationships between groups of people around the world. The students also learn how the society they live in evolved. Students discover the cause and effect of events and determine the relationships between them. Students also learn to understand current events in context with the past.

Today, students around the world have the opportunity to study history uncovered by archeologists. History class can be exciting and motivating to some students, while for other students, history may be uninteresting. The teacher influences student interest level by the subject matter and by the methods and style in which the teacher presents the topic to the class.

Tim, a high-school history teacher, met with Madeline, a student with Asperger Syndrome, and her family before the semester began. Since he had experience of working with students with Asperger Syndrome in the past, Tim wanted to take time to get to know Madeline and her family.

At the meeting with Madeline and her family, Tim gave her a packet of information concerning the content of the history class. He also told her the requirements needed to be successful in his class. This meeting gave the family time to process all of the requirements for the class. The meeting also afforded them the opportunity to get to know Tim, his expectations for the class work, and to begin planning for the semester. Tim benefited from this meeting by learning about the unique needs of Madeline, including her preferences and aversions.

Early in the semester, Tim assigned a nine-week genealogy project to the students. The purpose of the assignment was to encourage the students to understand that history is more than memorizing lists of dates, countries, wars, or leaders. Tim hoped that they would understand the effect of historical events on the lives of their ancestors. Tim's goal is to help the students realize that the social, political, and economic conditions of the time forced families to make drastic decisions for their survival.

Tim told the students to work independently on the project. However, the students were encouraged to interview different members of their family and to learn how the events of history affected and created their family history. They were also encouraged to use other sources from outside of the educational campus, such as online sources. Tim did not choose a group project because he knew this would cause Madeline a great deal of anxiety. Each student met with Tim throughout the semester to individualize the requirements for the final product. Tim knew that Madeline's parents provided tremendous assistance throughout the project.

Part of Madeline's final project consisted of videotaped stories told by her parents, siblings, grandparents, and one great-grandparent. With the assistance of her older brother, Madeline created a PowerPoint presentation using family pictures and favorite family music. Tim set up the computer and projection equipment and Madeline showed the video and the PowerPoint presentation to the students of the class.

At the end of the semester, Madeline's parents scheduled a meeting with Tim to discuss the semester's events. Madeline and her parents were grateful that Tim created a history project that Madeline was able to complete with assistance from her family. Madeline's parents told Tim that this was one of the few projects in Madeline's educational career that she felt pride in finishing. Madeline felt that, with Tim's and her parents' encouragement, she had done a great job.

Summary of strategies

1. Meet with the student with Asperger Syndrome prior to the start of the semester to get to know the student.

2. Plan projects that accommodate the student so he can be successful.

3. Provide differentiated instruction to suit the learning needs of each of the students in the classroom.

Points for reflection

1. How can a teacher meet the learning needs of a student with Asperger Syndrome in the classroom?

2. Are you willing to adjust your vision of a final project to accept what the student can do?

3. Should a teacher assist the student in presenting a final project to the class?

General testing

Teachers administer quizzes, tests, and exams to students to assess students' knowledge of a particular subject area. Types of assessments are often in the form of multiple choice, true/false, fill in the blanks, short answer, or essay questions.

Some school administrators and teachers have broadened the traditional testing methods to include grade-level benchmarks, classroom observations, learning stations, labs, portfolios, projects, and student interviews.

The purpose of the tests should be to provide performance data for analysis. This analysis can help a teacher or team of teachers to determine if the instruction has increased the students' base of knowledge and understanding of concepts taught from the curriculum. Teachers also use this information to verify that the material has been mastered. The teachers need to verify that the students have learned the material or to decide if there are areas of the curriculum that they need to teach further as part of the ongoing teaching/testing/teaching process. Testing data can help teachers plan appropriate lessons for the students. Parents receive report cards and attend conferences to keep them informed of student progress.

Students with Asperger Syndrome do not always express their full knowledge of learned subject matter on examinations. Some students may feel test anxiety due to the pressure they place upon themselves, the teacher emphasizing the importance of doing well on the test, or the type of exam that is being administered. Often, the student with Asperger Syndrome may feel more anxiety if the exam is in handwritten essay format, due to the student's problems with fine motor skills. School personnel, with parental input, need to address the unique testing requirements of students with Asperger Syndrome.

Tony, an eighth-grade student with Asperger Syndrome, becomes distracted when it is time for an assessment in any of his classes. Tony's health class teacher, William, noticed Tony's anxiety level began to rise when William began to discuss an upcoming exam or when the class was at the end of a chapter or unit because he knew a test would happen soon.

William arranged a meeting with Tony's parents and his team of teachers. William stated his concerns about Tony's anxiety, and the other team members agreed that Tony acted similarly in their classes. Tony's parents informed the team that it is difficult to motivate Tony to attend school on exam days.

The group created a plan of action to assist Tony in reducing his test anxiety. The team realized that Tony needed to have his individualized education plan revised by adding testing accommodations. These accommodations would ensure that Tony had an effective manner of expressing his knowledge of the subject area to his teachers. One accommodation that Tony would be given was that he would have extended time to complete exams. Added time would help Tony not feel pressured by and preoccupied with completion time. For exams with essay questions, Tony would have the assistance of a scribe to record his verbal answers. Tony needed a scribe because he had many creative ideas but his poor handwriting skills interfered with his ability to record these ideas on paper.

Next, his teacher placed blank monthly calendars in a special folder for Tony to record all of his test dates. The dates for class projects were not included on these calendars because completing the projects was not an issue with Tony. The teachers marked in the folder the anticipated date for future quizzes and tests along with the type of assessment it would be, such as essay, fill in the blanks, multiple choice, etc.

Tony understood that the test dates were estimates and the teacher could change the dates. At home each night, Tony and his mother reviewed the calendar and prepared for assessments a few days in advance. They completed and reviewed study guides created by each teacher. The study guides were formatted to be similar to the actual assessment. The teachers agreed not to ask for information in the assessment that was not contained in the study guide. The teachers also decided that if Tony performed poorly on an assessment, they would provide an opportunity for re-testing. In addition to the calendar, the team agreed that the guidance counselor would create a new "How to ACE Tests" group for students in Tony's grade.

The guidance counselor taught his "ACE" group strategies that would help them do well on exams. The students learned visualization and breathing activities to build their self-confidence and to create a positive attitude. The group also discussed the importance of keeping healthy by exercising regularly, getting enough sleep, and eating healthy foods.

Tony, a student who liked rules, understood the concept that he could do well on tests by following strategies that the guidance counselor gave him. Each student in the ACE group created a test-taking plan. Tony decided to begin each test by placing notes of any outline, lists, or formula that he may need for the test in the margin of the test.

Next, he decided to answer the questions on the tests that he thought were the easiest. Tony also included in his plan to remember to take time for slow deep breaths and to close his eyes and visualize not only the material he studied, but also himself doing well on the assessment. Tony knew that if he did not have enough time during the testing session he could request extended time during his study hall period.

MaryAnn, Tony's music teacher, gave her students a test on counting the beats in a measure and continuing the pattern to rhythms. Tony did poorly on the exam and MaryAnn shared the test with Tony's parents and the team. MaryAnn learned from Tony's mom that Tony does poorly in mathematics. MaryAnn realized that the skill that she taught the students in music class was based on the mathematics concepts of counting and adding numbers together. MaryAnn worked with the special education teacher to re-teach the material to Tony in a way that he understood. An adapted assessment was administered to Tony and he did well.

Summary of strategies

1. Find ways to relieve test anxiety as it can lead to poor performance on assessments.

2. Accommodations are essential to students' success on assessments. These can include:

    - extended time
    - a scribe
    - study guides
    - retaking the test
    - explaining the curriculum differently to the student so he understands the material better.

3. If a student becomes very anxious about "test talk," make provisions for the student to leave the room during test-taking discussions.

4. Teach the student how to take exams by creating an "exam-taking workshop."

Points for reflection

1. What are some of the signs that the student may be experiencing test anxiety?

2. Do you notice that other students in addition to students with Asperger Syndrome experience test-taking anxiety?

3. Are there any ways that you could lessen anxiety about tests for the entire class?

4. Are testing accommodations so critical that the teacher needs to include them in a formal individualized education plan?

5. Does the school staff need to teach the student strategies regarding how to take assessments?

6. Are you careful to ensure that you are testing the student on material that he is expecting?

Standardized assessments

Schools are under pressure to make sure that students make academic progress. School administrators use school-wide standardized testing to judge this progress. Performing well on these tests is a challenge to students with Asperger Syndrome.

Andrew is an eighth-grade student with Asperger Syndrome who does well academically with accommodations in the classroom. Andrew's teachers prepared him to take the required school-wide assessment. Andrew's accommodations include that he may take the test with no other students present, in a quiet setting, with an aide scribing his answers.

The day before the exam, Andrew felt physically ill and the teacher sent Andrew to the nurse to be examined. The nurse notified Andrew's mother that Andrew had a normal temperature but looked pale and sick.

After Andrew arrived home, his mother talked to him about his illness. Andrew said that he was upset about the assessment scheduled to take place the next day. Andrew told his mother that the principal talked on the morning announcements about doing well on the tests. The principal said that the students who perform poorly on the tests would have consequences, such as not being able to choose certain classes at the high school next year. Andrew felt that the principal was speaking directly to him and pressuring him to do well. Therefore, Andrew felt anxiety and fear regarding taking the assessment. Andrew's mother reviewed all standardized testing information that the school staff sent home to parents. She did not find any information in the letter that explained to parents or students that the results would determine the student's schedule for next year. Prior to the assessment the next morning, Andrew, his mother, and the principal talked.

The principal explained to Andrew that he wanted him to do his very best on the test. He reassured Andrew that the team would decide Andrew's schedule at his year-end individualized education plan conference. The team would base Andrew's high-school schedule on his needs and not on the results of the assessment. Andrew felt relieved after the conversation with the principal, and he began his first assessment that morning. Andrew's mother and the principal decided that, for future assessments, the principal would have a talk with Andrew after he made any announcements about school-wide assessments.

Sample standardized testing accommodations include:

- scheduled extended time

- scheduled breaks

- preferential seating

- testing in a separate room

- small group testing

- use of a calculator when permitted

- use of word processors

- dictation to a scribe

- simplifying and repeating directions

- reading aloud directions when permitted.

Summary of strategies

1. Investigate and implement a plan for standardized testing accommodations in the student's individualized education program.

2. Inform parents and students of all motivators and consequences of the results of testing.

3. Remove the student from discussions about standardized testing either in the classroom or in the general population through announcements.

4. Privately discuss school-wide testing with the student and the parent in an environment where the student can freely ask questions.

Points for reflection

1. What other accommodations may help a student with Asperger Syndrome on standardized school-wide assessments?

2. Would motivators help a student on such assessments?

3. Will the student benefit from knowing the consequences of doing well or poorly on a test?

CHAPTER 3

Special Subjects

Many school special education consultants overlook the need for accommodations for students with Asperger Syndrome during special subjects, such as art class. However, subjects such as art, music, and physical education present many challenges for the student with Asperger Syndrome.

These subjects, although not academic, involve the student using his senses in a way that could cause difficulty. For example, music class can present a great challenge for a student who has an aversion to loud noises. A music class can cause a meltdown for a student with Asperger Syndrome, given the loud noises and expectation to participate musically. A student with Asperger Syndrome may find music class intolerable without some appropriate accommodations. Similar difficulties could arise in art, physical education, and any other special class.

Additionally, the special classes present social challenges for the student with Asperger Syndrome. These classes are usually less structured than the academic classes and there is more peer interaction. Since the student with Asperger Syndrome has difficulty with both unstructured time and socialization, these classes can cause the student stress and anxiety.

Since these classes provide a break from the rigorous academic routine of the school day, it is important that teachers make accommodations for the student with Asperger Syndrome so that these classes can be fun and relaxing. Additionally, these classes can be excellent opportunities to provide the student with a structured environment in which to learn and practice socialization skills. Teachers may be unfamiliar with making accommodations for students with Asperger Syndrome in their "special" classes. However, with some thought and planning, accommodations do not need to be too difficult to devise and implement.

Art

Although art is not an academic subject, art class can be challenging for a student with Asperger Syndrome. The student has trouble following multiple-step directions. Many times, the art teacher verbally gives the directions for a project instead of writing them down, and the student cannot remember or follow the steps needed to complete the project. Additionally, art class projects involve using many different substances and textures that could affect a student with Asperger Syndrome. For example, the student may have sensitive fingertips and not be able to tolerate the feeling of sand on his fingers. This sensitivity would make it difficult for the student to make a drip castle made of sand. The student would probably get rather upset, both because he is unable to do the project and because the sand feels so uncomfortable to him. It is imperative that the art teacher consider the student's sensory difficulties when designing projects for the class.

The art teacher needs to know that the student has Asperger Syndrome. She also needs information concerning the student's sensory difficulties. If she is aware of this information, she can make the necessary accommodations to help the student with Asperger Syndrome be successful. Many times, the changes can be small, but they make a drastic difference to the student struggling to understand how to do a project.

Jessica is an art teacher at the elementary-school level. She knew Ali has Asperger Syndrome and had overheard Ali comment several times that he "hated art class." Jessica read over Ali's file and talked to his teacher. The teacher informed Jessica that Ali could not follow lengthy directions, had organization difficulties, and had very weak muscle tone, especially in his hands and fingers. The teacher told Jessica that Ali was very creative, but easily frustrated. When he got frustrated, Ali clapped his hands together quickly and made disruptive noises.

Jessica thought about ways to help Ali enjoy art more than he had in the past. First, she considered the next project that she had on her curriculum, which was for her students to make something out of clay. She decided that because the texture of the modeling clay may be too hard for Ali to use easily, she would allow Ali to use white Play-Doh™. He would be able to manipulate this material more easily and be less frustrated than if he used regular clay. She chose white Play-Doh™ because it was the most similar in appearance to the clay and would not make Ali stand out from the other students.

Jessica decided that she would write the directions on a large flip pad and place it on an easel where all the students could see it. She put one direction for the project on each sheet of paper. When Jessica explained the project, she went through the directions using the flip pad. Jessica told the class that after she was finished the directions would remain on the easel so anyone who needed to refresh his or her memory would be able to do so.

After hearing that some students with Asperger Syndrome have poor muscle tone, Jessica thought that the stools in the room would be uncomfortable for Ali. The stools do not have backs and are higher than regular chairs. Jessica gave all the students the option of using a regular desk chair and desk, and she assembled a group of four desks in the corner of the room. In that way, any student who became fatigued or uncomfortable sitting on the stools would be able to switch his or her seating. Ali felt much more comfortable sitting on the desk chairs and several of his classmates often joined him.

After these accommodations had been made for Ali, he started to enjoy art class. He especially liked when Jessica permitted the students to form their own creations out of the clay. Since Ali liked video-game characters, he made a detailed character from a video game and gave a brief presentation to the class about his project.

Summary of strategies

1. Get to know the student with Asperger Syndrome and his sensitivities that may influence his success in art class.

2. Do not hesitate to modify materials used on a project to make the student with Asperger Syndrome feel less anxious.

3.   Be sure that the seating in the room is as comfortable as possible.

4.   Write the directions for the project simply and clearly. Do not overwhelm the student with too many directions.

5.   Choose projects that you think the student with Asperger Syndrome will enjoy.

Points for reflection

1.   Have you considered that special classes, such as art and music, can be just as difficult at times as academic subjects for many students?

2.   What other materials could cause problems for students with tactile sensitivities? What might be good substitutes for these particular materials?

3.   Do you feel that, by making accommodations to the materials and the way that you present directions for the project, you are helping the student with Asperger Syndrome? Perhaps you believe that you may be doing him a disservice by making these accommodations.

Family and consumer science

In multi-ability classrooms, the teacher needs to be able to differentiate instruction to meet the various needs of learners in her classroom. The accommodations made for family and consumer science in this section are for cooking and sewing lessons. In some cooking classrooms, teachers assign students to groups or "families" to complete activities, where each student has a role to play in the family. For a student with Asperger Syndrome, the family task oriented concept may be difficult due to the amount of socialization required to be successful in such a group. Additionally, because the grade of the group depends on each person's ability within the group, the student with Asperger Syndrome may feel undue pressure to perform.

Students observe a cooking demonstration by the teacher, and the teacher asks the students to make the same product. The family assigns each member tasks to complete. Teachers grade the students on not only their final product, but also how they function in the group.

As part of the family, the students need to be able to read and follow the directions on the recipe. Then, the students need to do their part of the recipe when it is their turn. Since the grade depends in large part on the social interaction, the student with Asperger Syndrome may worry that the other students will blame him if he makes a mistake and the group does not get a good grade. The student with Asperger Syndrome can have feelings of pressure and anxiety. These feelings can cause him to have negative feelings about himself and can lead to a meltdown.

Nisha, a family and consumer science middle-school teacher, has had Jonathan, a student with Asperger Syndrome, in her class since sixth grade. Nisha understands her non-academic class can be quite a challenge for Jonathan in many ways. Nisha collaborates with Jonathan's team of teachers to create a family group that would best suit Jonathan's needs. Nisha sends home the recipes for the semester to Jonathan's mom in advance so the family can review and practice the tasks at home. She also communicates frequently with Jonathan's mom so they can monitor progress together and follow up on areas in which he has difficulty.

For the first cooking assignment, Jonathan's goal was to stir the ingredients of the recipe. The stirring can be a challenge for Jonathan because he has some dexterity problems. Nisha sent home the exact bowl and stirring utensils. Having the ingredients at home allows Jonathan to practice the skill and increase his speed. Jonathan was very nervous and worried about having to stir the ingredients. He felt that he was very slow. However, since he practiced at home with his mother, he became adept at using the cooking utensils and increased his speed using the utensils. Jonathan got used to the feeling of mixing the ingredients and working at greater speeds. He was then able to mix ingredients quickly in class.

The teachers grade the students on the speed in which they finish the recipe, because class time is limited. Since he had practiced at home and he knew what the recipe was about, Jonathan kept up with the group. The group praised Jonathan's skill in doing his part of the recipe. Jonathan felt camaraderie with the group. Nisha realized that students learn more than cooking skills in her class. Jonathan learned that preparation is important to success and that appropriate social interaction feels good.

The sewing portion of the class also challenged Jonathan. Jonathan was much less familiar with sewing than with cooking. He had never used a needle and thread. Jonathan's hands and fingers have low muscle tone. He had never mastered using scissors.

First, Nisha gave Jonathan a limited number of patterns to choose one from, all using easy cutting and sewing techniques, and with large pieces that would make the cutting and sewing easier. She chose patterns that incorporated wheels and cars, as these were interesting to Jonathan. She was able to find several suitable patterns, which also had simple directions. Nisha provided Jonathan with needles with large eyes. Jonathan also has needles available at home for him to practice threading.

Summary of strategies

1.   Prior to cooking, the teacher can instruct students on family/ group dynamics as part of the lesson unit.

2.   Reinforce the need for cooperation and encouragement of the family group.

3.   Send home copies of recipes to practice skills at home. Parents can inform the teacher of the skills that the student with Asperger Syndrome can perform easily.

4.   Select an appropriate group in which to place the student with Asperger Syndrome.

5.   Select sewing patterns that have simple directions and large pieces so the student can cut and sew with ease.

6.   Provide sewing needles with large eyes to assist in needle threading tasks.

Points for reflection

1. What other accommodations can the family and consumer science teacher provide that will help the student with Asperger Syndrome to flourish?

2. Is there a way to teach members of the group to be sensitive to the needs of students with Asperger Syndrome in this class?

3. Can you provide alternatives to the assignments through differentiated instruction to help students with and without difficulties in this class?

4. What are the desired outcomes of the family and consumer science curriculum?

Physical education

Since many students with Asperger Syndrome have poor muscle tone and coordination, and gross motor deficits, physical education may be one of the most challenging classes for these students. Physical education is also a challenge for students with Asperger Syndrome because the class involves numerous opportunities for social interaction and team activities. Physical education teachers need to be aware of these students' particular strengths and weaknesses. The teachers can then tailor the gym class to better suit these students' needs as well as to encourage physical activity. Physical education teachers can use some simple strategies to keep the student attending and participating in gym class.

Sarah is a high-school physical education teacher. She learned that students with Asperger Syndrome need routines to get through potentially difficult moments. She also learned that these students need visual cues to help them make sense of their classes. The strategies she uses for students with Asperger Syndrome work very well with the rest of her students in her class. The strategies help all students stay focused on activities and increase participation.

Sarah requires that her students meet at the same place in the gym for each class. These students have the same partner for all the physical education class activities that require partners. In order to assure a good match for partners, Sarah reviews each student's record and observes the students for the first few classes. She chooses partners for the students with Asperger Syndrome based on their personalities. She selects partners who show compassion towards others. She also tries to choose someone who the student with Asperger Syndrome knew prior to the physical education class.

Sarah asked other teachers about their opinion regarding appropriate gym partners. She discovered that choosing the right partner for the student with Asperger Syndrome can help reduce the student's anxiety and helps him to enjoy physical education class. By assigning partners at the beginning of the school year, Sarah considerably reduced the anxiety of all students, since being chosen last is a concern for everyone.

Sarah has a large whiteboard that is visible to all students in the class. The board lists the activities for the day, broken down into ten-minute intervals. This board and schedule serve two purposes. They provide a structure for the class that is visible to all students, so the student with Asperger Syndrome will not feel confused even if the level of noise and activity in the gym increases. Additionally, the schedule can provide reassurance for the student with Asperger Syndrome. If the student does not like the activity or feels it to be overwhelming, at least he will know when it will be over.

At the beginning of the class, Sarah explains the purpose of each of the activities. After explaining the plan for each class period, she, or one of her students, demonstrates how to do the activities for the class period.

There is a short practice session so Sarah can make sure all students know what is required for the gym period. The student with Asperger Syndrome, in addition to having a gym partner for the physical activities, may have an aide to assist if needed. If the student is having a tough time, the aide brings the student out in the hallway to cool down, to take a drink, or to talk. Sarah knows that she has to strike a balance between placing demands on her student with Asperger Syndrome and adjusting expectations so the student does not feel overwhelmed.

As part of the physical education curriculum, Sarah also gives out text regarding the rules and history of the particular sports in which the students are engaging. Sarah feels that providing all the students with concrete knowledge about the rules of the games and the history of the sport increases the students' interest in physical education.

Sarah noticed that students with Asperger Syndrome have trouble concentrating when there are loud noises in the gym. Often the level of noise is high, especially when the class is involved in playing an indoor sport. Sarah tries a few different strategies to assist students with Asperger Syndrome in this regard. First, she gives the entire class a warning if she feels that the activity will be especially noisy on a particular day. She also built into the daily class "quiet breaks" in which the students stop the activity and cool down by walking around the gym silently.

Sometimes a student with Asperger Syndrome responds to excessive noise by placing his hands over his ears and squeezing his eyes closed. On particularly noisy days, Sarah watches for this type of behavior. If she sees that the student is in distress, she has the classroom aide take him into the hallway to avoid him feeling over-stimulated. Although Sarah tries to plan her classes to reduce noise, she is comfortable making accommodations, particularly if a student cannot cope with the sensory input. Sarah realizes that students with Asperger Syndrome may not be able to participate in every activity. She adjusts her expectations and requirements of such students accordingly.

Sarah also has some other creative ideas about how to reduce noise in the gym so students with Asperger Syndrome can participate in class. During one class, she challenged her students to play a game of volleyball in total silence. Her students enjoyed this change in routine. The only noise that the students made throughout this activity was laughter.

Sarah tries to vary the activities that the students participate in each day and the noise level varies with the class. She finds that students enjoy the variety. Her students with Asperger Syndrome do not dread, and in fact enjoy, physical education classes with her.

Swimming

Sarah's students have the option of choosing a swim class instead of regular physical education. The students can choose to take up to two sessions of swimming per week. Sarah had read that many students with Asperger Syndrome enjoy swimming, because is a non-competitive activity that does not require a great deal of muscle strength. Additionally, some students with Asperger Syndrome seem to feel more coordinated in the water than on a gym floor.

Sarah's students with Asperger Syndrome are sometimes hesitant at first to try swimming. However, Sarah has a very good gym aide. She and her aide are able to give personalized attention to each student in teaching basic swimming strokes.

The students with Asperger Syndrome usually began to love the water. They reported that it is good to be in the water because it feels so relaxing. Since her students with Asperger Syndrome do so well in the water, Sarah often permits the students to take the maximum number of swim classes allowed. The students learn to swim well enough to perform some of the easier strokes. The students also like to do laps around the pool by walking around in the water. Swimming is usually a positive experience for students with Asperger Syndrome.

Summary of strategies

1.   Use similar routines for each class session.

2.   Try to vary noise levels with each class. Try some silent activities for a student challenge.

3.   Allow the student to take a break if needed. Try to have a classroom aide available for breaks.

4.   Include students' interests in lessons, for example, by incorporating the history of sports in some lessons.

5.   Use a whiteboard for visual cues to keep the students informed of the schedule for the class.

6.   Demonstrate the activity at the beginning of each class.

7.   Investigate whether or not swimming is available for the student.

Points for reflection

1.   Is there a particular sport you enjoyed as a student?

2.   Can you imagine the feelings of a student who has both gross motor difficulties as well as social skills problems in a gym class?

3.   Do you encourage all students to participate in the gym class while making accommodations for the students who are less athletic?

Computers

For many students, computers are a great source of information and a way to access games and fun software. Students with Asperger Syndrome often have positive experiences with computers as well. However, computers can cause problems for these students for a few reasons. The students' fine motor difficulties can make typing at the keyboard tedious and uncomfortable.

Some students have difficulty using online resources because of the visual difficulty. Computer screens often show a great deal of colors, variety of website page formats, and mixed use of font sizes and types. Accessing websites, emails, file servers, etc., requires many different user inputs. In addition, search engines operate differently from one another. Students with Asperger Syndrome may find the online experience to be overwhelming because of these visual-spatial issues.

Carmela, a middle-school computer teacher, learned about this issue when one of her students, who receives good grades and is very cooperative and helpful, was having a difficult time using the computer in her lab. Carmela knew that Hannah has Asperger Syndrome. However, no one told Carmela or could explain why Hannah had difficulty using the computer. Hannah's occupational therapist explained to Carmela about the disorder and the difficulty that Hannah has with writing. Carmela worked with Hannah on the computer and found that she had trouble finding information on the page. However, she had no problems using a simple word-processing program. The word-processing program was helpful, since it reduced Hannah's need to handwrite. Carmela and the occupational therapist devised a simple strategy for Hannah to use when she needed to use the computer for tasks other than word processing. They realized that they needed to structure Hannah's experience to make the computer seem less confusing and easier to navigate visually.

Carmela gave Hannah a cardboard "window" to use. This is a small piece of cardboard with a rectangular hole approximately 2" × 3" cut out. Hannah uses this when scanning information on the computer monitor. The cardboard cutout allows Hannah to look for information in smaller areas at a time. This card is particularly helpful when looking for information on a website.

To access different programs on the computer, Carmela made software "shortcuts" so that Hannah can simply point and click on icons representing different software programs. Hannah uses these shortcuts as opposed to having to search through menus to find such programs.

A peer buddy was "trained" and assigned to assist Hannah during the computer class. Carmela found several volunteers who wanted to work with Hannah, so finding a peer helper was not a problem. Hannah has one peer buddy to ensure there is consistency in the help that is given to her. The peer helper was "trained" by simply explaining the difficulty Hannah has on the computer. Hannah also explained to her peer helper when she has the most difficult time.

Since Carmela implemented these simple strategies, Hannah has begun to enjoy working on the computer. Hannah can now explain to other teachers about the accommodations that she needs.

Summary of strategies

1. Obtain the services of other professionals (e.g. occupational therapist) when it is unclear how to help a student with Asperger Syndrome.

2. For students with Asperger Syndrome with visual-spatial problems, limit the amount of visual information presented, whether in written assignments or on the computer.

3. Peer helpers are an excellent way to help students with Asperger Syndrome without having them stand out from other students. Peer helpers can be trained simply and easily for working with students with Asperger Syndrome.

Points for reflection

1. Can you recall the best websites that you visited, and what you liked most about them?

2. When you have difficulty with an assignment or task, do you obtain help from peers at work or in the neighborhood? Is there a colleague who you rely upon frequently? How may this be like having a peer helper?

Driver education

Most parents worry when their student begins to learn to drive. Parents of students with Asperger Syndrome worry quite a bit when the student reaches driving age. While many individuals with Asperger Syndrome have no difficulty learning to drive a car, others may need a great deal of instruction and practice to operate a motor vehicle safely. The opportunity to drive a car is important for the independence of any individual. Driver education is a course offered by many schools. Students with Asperger Syndrome who are planning to learn to drive should take such a course.

Individuals with Asperger Syndrome often learn to follow rules concretely. This characteristic of these students can help them to learn how to drive since there are many rules to driving and following the law.

Distractions cause between 20 and 30 percent of all automobile accidents according to the United States National Highway Traffic Safety Administration (Shelton 2001). This is important because individuals with Asperger Syndrome may have more problems with distractions.

Some students with Asperger Syndrome have difficulty with visual-spatial tasks. Those that do may have the most significant difficulty driving. Driving uses many skills, including a person being able to focus on driving, and responding immediately to changes in the environment. Changes in the environment can include a change in weather, a car stopping suddenly in front of your car, and other unpredictable variables. From a safety perspective, it is important that a team of professionals complete an assessment for students with Asperger Syndrome who would like to drive. The team needs to assess the visual-motor tasks, distractibility, and gross motor skills of the student.

The assessment can be conducted by a team of professionals and can include a school psychologist, occupational therapist, and driver education teacher, among others. Once the student is assessed and is believed to be capable of learning to operate a motor vehicle, and the student is of the proper age, driver education training may begin.

Graham, a driver education teacher, found out about Ravi's disorder after Ravi enrolled in his class. The experiential part of driver education begins after several weeks of study in Graham's classroom. Ravi's parents were surprised to find out that Ravi had enrolled for the course. Ravi had expressed his interest in the class to his guidance counselor. The guidance counselor approved the course after speaking with his teachers and occupational therapist. Ravi's parents were pleased that the school staff thought he had the abilities to learn how to drive.

Ravi never had trouble with visual-spatial tasks and followed school rules well. Ravi's parents and Graham were more concerned with Ravi's reaction to everyday occurrences with which drivers have to deal, such as children running out from a sidewalk. Graham decided that Ravi would receive an added amount of time in training, plus a new component regarding handling emergency maneuvers. Ravi was provided with approximately double the amount of the experiential portion of the driver education course. Graham devised strategies to teach and test emergency maneuvers repeatedly. Simulated situations on an empty parking lot included the following and required both emergency breaking and avoidance steering:

- stroller (with doll) rolled in front of Ravi's car
- obstacle course
- water sprayed on windshield while driving
- loud music playing
- driving with a flat tire
- driving over objects (e.g. branches, balls)
- focus on driving and ignoring distractions.

Ravi's parents and Graham made Ravi practice emergency breaking and avoidance procedures until he responded to many different situations calmly and effectively. Ravi passed his course and his official driver's test. Ravi's parents still work with him on responding to emergencies. Ravi still practices driving in empty parking lots to ensure that he remains comfortable driving, remaining alert to driving and responding to distractions, and handling unexpected driving experiences.

Ravi's parents and Graham agreed not to use computer simulation programs to prepare Ravi for on-the-road driving. Ravi plays computer games for fun. They felt that Ravi would not take driving seriously and would not generalize information from the computer to real-life experiences if he used a computer simulation. Additionally, Ravi's parents thought that the computer simulation might confuse him.

Summary of strategies

1. Over-prepare students for driving in the real world. Provide more practice opportunities.

2. Practice given simulated emergencies repeatedly.

3. Continue practicing emergency response maneuvers even after the student has passed his official driver's test.

4. If there is a question, arrange for the student to be assessed for readiness to learn how to drive by appropriate professionals.

Points for reflection

1. What prepared you most for learning how to drive?

2. What are the biggest distractions when you drive?

3. Have you ever had an accident, speeding ticket, etc.? Do you remember the cause?

4. What do you think students with Asperger Syndrome need to know as a prerequisite to driving?

5. What are other potentially dangerous activities for which we need to prepare students with Asperger Syndrome?

6. Will simulated driving computer programs be of assistance to other students with Asperger Syndrome?

Foreign languages

Foreign language class is a course that students are expected to take in many high schools. Colleges often require students to have taken several years of a foreign language before being accepted for admittance. Since the 1970s, the need for foreign language classes has grown. Businesses and government entities need individuals with skills in foreign languages for public relations and trade purposes. Job opportunities exist globally for those people who are bilingual and who understand the nuances of the culture in the country or region where people speak the particular language. Many organizations hire individuals who know the language of a particular country and also understand and appreciate the customs and beliefs of that country.

Students who study a foreign language begin to make connections and growth in English vocabulary once they learn that many words are derived from other languages. Students also learn an appreciation of other countries' art, music, and culture. Students of all abilities can benefit from exposure to foreign languages in schools.

Juan, a secondary Spanish educator, teaches conversational Spanish to high-school students. He uses a variety of teaching techniques in his classroom. Before signing up for Juan's class, Keith, a student with

Asperger Syndrome, talked with his guidance counselor about auditing one of Juan's Spanish classes. The guidance counselor showed Keith a video Juan had made of one of his class lessons. Keith was surprised when he saw Juan jumping around the room, heard Juan speaking loudly in Spanish, and heard the students reciting back answers to Juan in Spanish.

After watching the video for 15 minutes, Keith began to laugh at the excitement that he saw in the room. He wanted to see Juan in action in the classroom. Juan and Keith met several times before Keith came to observe the class. Keith felt comfortable with Juan, and he realized that Juan was a nice person who was a very energetic and enthusiastic teacher.

Keith entered the classroom before the other students. He sat close to the door, in case he needed to exit the room if it became too loud for him. The bell rang for class to begin, and Juan jumped into the center of the room yelling, "Hola!" The students shouted back, "Hola, Señor!" Juan and the students held a conversation back and forth in Spanish, which Juan repeated in English for the first few minutes of class. Juan then began the lesson of reviewing the Spanish cultural vocabulary and colloquialisms. After the review, the students formed two teams and played a game using a fly swatter and Spanish vocabulary. The class was buzzing with excitement as each of the students tried to swat the correct Spanish word on the board before his or her competitor did. When the game was finished, the students were given a worksheet to reinforce the vocabulary they had learned.

Keith was very attentive throughout the class. He became excited and flapped occasionally when the game being played was intense, but Keith felt the entire class was fun. After the class, Keith, Juan, and the guidance counselor talked about Keith's experience during the visitation. Keith decided to register for Juan's class with the understanding that if the class became too intense, Keith would be able to excuse himself from the room and come back after he was calm. Juan agreed to provide Keith with notes and vocabulary for the class a week ahead of time so Keith could preview the material. He also agreed to audiotape the class, so Keith could listen to the class at home if he needed reinforcement of the lesson.

Once the semester began, Keith adjusted to the volume and the intense action in the classroom. However, testing situations provided stress for Keith. Keith began to take his tests with Juan during a study hall period. Juan agreed that the first few paper and pen tests in the class did not reflect

Keith's true knowledge of the subject matter. Keith was also reluctant to complete oral tests on a tape recorder. Juan tested Keith on core concepts needed to meet the course objects orally one on one. Juan offered an alternative method of testing Keith without compromising the integrity of the course.

Summary of strategies

1. The student may need to observe the foreign language class prior to selecting the course.

2. The student and the teacher may need to build a personal relationship initially.

3. The student may need to be provided with written material in the form of class notes and vocabulary and an audiotape of the class period.

Points for reflection

1. Can the student benefit from the foreign language class experience?

2. Can the student audiotape the class for reinforcement purposes?

3. Can the teacher provide class notes and vocabulary to the student in written form?

4. Are there alternative tests available to assess student knowledge?

Music

Music classes are full of stimulation, variety, and changes. Sounds in music class vary from loud to soft and from high to low pitches. Playing a musical instrument requires the use of gross or fine motor skills. For students with sensory system sensitivities and with musculature difficulties, music class can be a very difficult experience.

Many students with Asperger Syndrome like music and music classes. Each student with Asperger Syndrome is different, and his needs are different as well. While this book attempts to address as many problems as possible, not all students with Asperger Syndrome have the same difficulties.

The principal informed Lewis, a music teacher at the middle-school level, that he would be having a new student who has Asperger Syndrome. Lewis' son has Asperger Syndrome and therefore Lewis has learned a great deal about the disorder. Lewis' new student, Stuart, was afraid of loud sounds. He also had trouble with excessive tactile stimulation when he tried to play different instruments. Stuart said that his hands felt "tingly" from the vibrations. Stuart enjoys singing and likes the stories revealed within songs. Lewis has asked his own son's school staff to make appropriate accommodations for him, so he was prepared to make accommodations for his students with special needs.

Lewis decided to assess Stuart's strengths and weaknesses in music prior to his attending music class. He asked Stuart about his favorite types of instruments and music. Stuart seemed afraid of coming to music class, so Lewis offered him some accommodations.

Lewis gave Stuart a written pass that Stuart can use when he feels over-stimulated. Stuart is able to leave class at will when the sounds feel too loud for him. Lewis began posting the activities that would take place during the class period, so Stuart could see the upcoming events and think ahead of time when he may want to leave. For example, Stuart cannot stand the sound of the triangle or the bells, and leaves class if there is a group activity using these instruments. Lewis gave Stuart a set of soft earplugs for use in class. There are several types of earplugs, each set with a different texture. Lewis let Stuart try different types until he settled on a pair of earplugs that were comfortable.

These simple accommodations helped to increase Stuart's participation in music class and have taken away much of the fear and anxiety of attending this class. Lewis always smiles at his students, including Stuart, when they enter the classroom. Many times Lewis asks Stuart how his day is going. Lewis believes that building a rapport with Stuart also helps him to feel comfortable and safe in music class.

Summary of strategies

1.   Assess the strengths and needs of the student with Asperger Syndrome, as well as his sound, music, and musical instrument preferences.

2.   Have the student use earplugs if necessary.

3.   List the class activities on the board.

4.   Allow the student with Asperger Syndrome to leave the classroom if needed.

5.   Build a rapport with the student with Asperger Syndrome so he feels comfortable in the classroom.

Points for reflection

1.   Did you enjoy music class in school?

2.   Do loud sounds bother you?

3.   How can the accommodations made by Lewis be helpful for other students without Asperger Syndrome?

4.   Why is it important to build a rapport with students with Asperger Syndrome?

CHAPTER 4

Other Periods in the School Day

There are many unstructured times during the school day. Although these periods are not usually a problem for students without disabilities, students with Asperger Syndrome may have difficulty figuring out how to handle these times. Some of these unstructured periods include the students transitioning from one class to the next, homeroom, waiting to get on a bus, and navigating hallways.

There are times during the school day that require the student with Asperger Syndrome to do several things quickly, without adequate opportunities for preparation. One way to make these transition times less stressful is to allow the student with Asperger Syndrome to leave class sooner than the other students. A peer helper can guide the student through hallways.

The student with Asperger Syndrome can learn to become independent and navigate unstructured times successfully using different types of accommodations. Learning to deal positively with transitions and unstructured time is a skill that can greatly help the student with Asperger Syndrome be successful throughout his life. It is important that he learn these skills while he is still in school.

Homeroom

Morning homeroom time can be very hectic in any school setting. After students have obtained all of their materials from their lockers for the morning classes, the "routine" of homeroom begins. Since the activities in homeroom are usually unstructured, the student with Asperger Syndrome feels upset by all the activity that needs to take place in a small amount of time. Students with Asperger Syndrome may feel over-whelmed. Their anxiety starts to build at this early time in the school day. In order for the student with Asperger Syndrome to feel calmer during the school day, the teacher needs to make accommodations during homeroom.

Homeroom is usually unstructured for students because they are preparing for their day by doing activities such as choosing a lunch, orga-nizing materials, voting for class officers, collecting cans for the food drive, listening to announcements, and reviewing the schedule for the day. Teachers are busy taking attendance, reviewing the schedule, answering student questions, and sending students to the office.

Laura, a high-school English teacher, has Mario, a freshman student with Asperger Syndrome, in her homeroom. Mario is poorly organized and impulsive. He also feels very sluggish in the mornings. The combina-tion of these characteristics makes it difficult for Mario to get his materials together for the school day. Mario's mother reports that she has difficulty getting him out of bed and that she has to prod him to get going in the morning. Mario needs extra help in homeroom to begin his day.

Laura was concerned about Mario and wanted her homeroom to run smoothly for all of her students. She sought the advice of other teachers to give her ideas to help Mario begin his day on a positive note. Laura allows Mario to come to homeroom five minutes early to organize his materials and review the schedule for the day. Since Laura is in the room at the time, she greets Mario and reminds him what he needs to do during homeroom.

Mario likes to talk about video games. In order to help Mario make the transition to function effectively during the school day, Laura asks Mario to tell her something new about a video game. The rule is that Mario needs to limit his talking to about two minutes and then he needs to focus on his schedule for the day. Mario looks forward to telling Laura what is new in video games. The conversations about his interest help Mario feel livelier in the mornings. The dialogue with Laura, in addition to helping Mario be acclimated to the school day, helps Laura and Mario establish a good relationship. Mario has someone to talk to about the stresses of school and to help him handle difficult moments.

Mario is aware of any special changes to the daily schedule, because Laura provided Mario's parents with special bell schedules for any school delays and any special activities that may happen in the school. These activities include voting, collecting items, door-decorating contests, and participating in school-wide activities. Laura sends Mario's parents an updated schedule and event calendar weekly. Mario's mother reviews these schedule changes and contacts Laura if she has any questions. Mario's mother also explains special activities to Mario. Mario is permitted to decide whether he wishes to participate in these activates.

Laura begins each homeroom class by setting a timer for two minutes. The principal has agreed to delay the onset of announcements. During these two minutes, the students know that the teacher takes attendance, finalizes lunch count, and reviews the bell schedule. The teacher does not issue student passes at this time. Students perform special activities, such as voting, after the announcements are completed. After announcements, all the students, including Mario, know they need to be attentive to Laura as she provides other pertinent information to the students. After the routine tasks are completed, the students prepare to leave for their first class.

Previously, Mario had a problem with the noise level in the classroom. When it was excessively noisy in the room, he would hold his ears and sway slightly. Laura noticed his discomfort and adjusted the volume of the announcements to a comfortable level for all students. This small adjustment in volume helped Mario considerably.

By Mario coming into homeroom early and having a short period of quiet time to look at the schedule, and by a consistent routine implemented by Laura, Mario's days have been less stressful for him. The homeroom routine helps Mario start the day in a good frame of mind.

Summary of strategies

1. Create a structured consistent homeroom period.

2. Allow a student with Asperger Syndrome extra time in the morning to prepare for the day.

3. Review special bell schedules with the students.

4. Inform parents about special homeroom and school-wide activities.

5. Keep the noise level of announcements to a level comfortable for students.

6. Find a way to establish a rapport with the student with Asperger Syndrome to show him you are glad to see him each day.

Points for reflection

1. How can you make the homeroom period structured so that the student and you can do the daily tasks with a minimum of rushing and stress?

2. Do you post the schedule for the day clearly in a consistent area for all students to view?

3. Is there a way you could make the homeroom period a time of respite for the students to prepare themselves for their day?

4. Students, including those with Asperger Syndrome, are aware of the feelings of others (for example, a hurried teacher). How can you structure your morning to feel less rushed?

Hallways

The hallways in any junior high, middle, or high school function as a time for unstructured group interaction with many unspoken socialization rules. Hallways provide little space for students to open lockers, congregate with friends, and move to their next period.

The noise volume in this space can be quite loud with students talking and with announcements blaring over the public address system. In addition, inappropriate student interactions occur during the time in the hallways. Some student actions that can occur in hallways include jabbing, pushing, bullying, eating, and public displays of affection. School personnel may not fully enforce school rules at this time. The lack of rule enforcement may be because the students greatly outnumber the teachers. One student with Asperger Syndrome called the hallways "the lawless town."

For a student with Asperger Syndrome, the hallways may provide sensory overload. The student may worry about bullies or about the pressure of getting to his destination. During hallway times, the student may also think about time limitations, and the lack of order and rules. Not only does the physical proximity of one body against another body provide too much physical stimulation, but also the playful jabbing, bumping, and flicking between peers can lead to a student with Asperger Syndrome to behave inappropriately. This misbehavior may result in a disciplinary referral or maladaptive behaviors such as flapping. Unfortunately, the school does not provide a class titled "Hallways 101." School staff members expect students to understand how to behave in the hallways by learning unwritten social rules.

Ian, a sophomore, is a new transfer student into Hazel's high-school computer class. Hazel began having problems with Ian in the first week of school when he was late to class, asked to use the restroom every day, and was not focused on the lessons.

Hazel's frustration with Ian led her to discuss Ian's behavior with the principal and Ian's guidance counselor. Hazel also consulted with Ian's special education teacher. The team held a meeting with all of Ian's teachers and his mother to discover what events were causing stress for Ian at school. After the meeting, the guidance counselor, George, followed Ian through the building to track his actions outside of instructional class time. George followed Ian from the time he exited the bus to the time he re-entered the bus at the end of the day. George discovered that Ian had a difficult time finding his way around the building and literally bounced off one student to the next as he attempted to maneuver his way through the hallways to his classes.

After reviewing George's notes, the team created a plan for Ian to help him to navigate the hallways. The plan would help Ian be better prepared both mentally and physically for his classes.

Each of Ian's teachers released Ian from class two minutes early so he could proceed to his next class. Ian did not need to schedule a locker break since the teachers kept an extra set of books in the classroom for him. George and Ian mapped out a route for Ian to follow to each of his classes. The route included a restroom and drink break.

Since Ian arrived at his next class as the other students were leaving, he was able to get his books ready on his desk and write the homework assignment from the board into his agenda book before class started. Ian was also able to eat a quick snack in the room before the other students arrived. The teachers noticed a dramatic improvement in Ian's demeanor since the new system was put into place.

Halfway through the semester, the team reconvened and felt that Ian was ready to be challenged and reintegrated into the hallways. Ian had several meetings with George to learn the rules of the hallways. George videotaped the interactions of the students in the hallway. The videotape allowed George to teach Ian the procedures of hallway etiquette. Ian did not understand that most of the students in the hallway who touched him were not intending to harm him.

George and Ian watched the videotape of students bumping into each other and some students playing with each other physically. George taught Ian to tell others "Stop!" if he was pushed or bumped purposely by other students. Ian practiced this technique at school and at home.

George also gathered a group of peer helpers to practice walking closely together and bumping each other. Ian saw this as a fun and humorous activity. He began to realize that the physical contact was not going to hurt him and most of the time was not done on purpose.

George taught Ian that sometimes students bully others in the hallways and that Ian needs to report bullying to an adult in the building as soon as the bullying occurs. George also instructed Ian not to join his peers when they behave in inappropriate ways, such as yelling or throwing things. Ian told George that a school staff member always catches Ian when he misbehaves at school. Ian explained that he does these behaviors because the other students have told him to do so. George taught Ian to be assertive and say "No!" in such circumstances.

After several sessions, George and Ian stood in a small landing in the hallway as the students traveled during hallway times. Ian stood closely to George and listened to the noises in the hall. He felt safe next to George. After Ian was comfortable with the noise levels, he and George began to walk the crowded hallways with George taking the lead, "blocking" for Ian. After Ian felt comfortable with being in the hallway with George, Ian's friend, who had the same schedule, assisted Ian in navigating his way to his next class. This plan took time to develop and implement. However, this plan had a positive impact in the long term for Ian. Ian no longer needs his peers or teachers to assist him in the hallways. Ian had not wanted to attend school because of this hallway issue. He now sees school as a safe place with many caring individuals.

Summary of strategies

1. Students with Asperger Syndrome need assistance in overcoming anxiety about noise levels, which can be very loud in many hallways.

2. Students with Asperger Syndrome also need assistance with overcoming any aversion to other students touching or bumping into them in hallways.

3. Students with Asperger Syndrome can benefit from learning the rules of the hallway and procedures to follow if someone bumps into them or bullies them.

4. Students may be constrained by time to go to the locker, use the restroom, and get to class on time and may need additional time to do so.

Points for reflection

1. Can you think of other experiences in school that would make a student with Asperger Syndrome not like school?

2. Why do students often bully students with Asperger Syndrome?

3. Is it the job of school staff to teach a student how to navigate hallways?

Lunch

Lunch is a noisy, unstructured time in many schools. Lunchtime at school is inherently full of stimulation including tastes, textures, sounds, and smells. Students with Asperger Syndrome have trouble with their sensory systems. Therefore, it makes sense that the lunch period can be a very difficult part of the school day for these students.

Rebecca is a lunch aide in an elementary school. She noticed that Said had difficulty during lunch. Often, Said would sit alone and he would not eat anything during the lunch period. Said would not communicate what was wrong when Rebecca asked him, and she became concerned. She talked with Said's teacher who informed her about Said's Asperger Syndrome.

Not knowing anything about Asperger Syndrome, Rebecca looked online for information. She also read a copy of Said's special accommodations. As Rebecca learned abut the characteristics of Asperger Syndrome, she realized that Said has a tough time with transitions from place to place and with loud noises. Said's parents told Rebecca that they give Said a modified diet because Said has specific food preferences. For example, Said does not like different foods to touch each other on a plate. He also does not like spicy foods and many kinds of meats.

Rebecca realized that the school staff had not anticipated Said's lunch period to be a problem for him. The staff probably overlooked any potential problems because Said never complained at lunch and he sat quietly.

Said's teacher and Rebecca sat down with Said's parents to discuss the situation. This team suggested a few things that they would like to try. They gave Said a schedule for the lunch period. This schedule does not list actual times, but rather includes a sequence of events, as Said's teacher reported that in class, Said watched the clock quite often, and was frequently overly concerned about getting tasks done on time. The schedule has been memorized by Said.

Said's schedule:

1. Go with Rebecca to lunch before the other students.
2. Pick out the lunch items from the counter.
3. Pay for lunch.

4. Sit in Section B.

5. Eat slowly and, if you wish, talk with Rebecca.

6. When you are ready, return your tray to the cleaning line. If you need more time to eat, you may take all the time you need.

7. Time to return to homeroom.

Said goes to lunch about a minute before the class with a peer partner. Said can pick out his preferred lunch items without feeling rushed and without the noise and stimulation of crowds. Said sits in a quieter part of the lunchroom with his peer partner. Other students are welcome to sit with Said.

Said's anxiety about finishing his meal in time had resulted in his losing his appetite. The staff agreed to let Said know that he can have all the time he needs to finish. Said is a good-natured, well-mannered student, and the staff knew that Said would not purposely take advantage of this opportunity (e.g. miss his next class by claiming that he needed more time to eat). The principal informed the lunch staff of Said's special needs and they were anxious to help. The lunch staff had also been concerned that Said was not eating during lunchtime.

Said is now eating his lunch and has begun conversing with Cheri, his peer partner. He still feels anxious at times during the lunch period, which results in his eating very little. Rebecca monitors Said and, during these stressful times, she will talk with him. She usually reminds Said that he has all the time he needs to eat. Sometimes she sits in the lunchroom with him to talk.

Rebecca's concern about Said's lunchtime was quite appropriate. She took the initiative to make him feel more comfortable and to eat a meal with her. Good nutrition at lunch is important for learning. After a good meal, Said is able to function more effectively for the remainder of the school day.

Summary of strategies

1. Give the student a schedule for the lunch period.

2. Use a peer partner to assist.

3.   Help students feel less anxious during the lunch period to reduce the chance that they will not have an appetite to eat.

4.   Inform lunch staff of students with special needs.

5.   Work in a team to find solutions to problems experienced by students with Asperger Syndrome.

Points for reflection

1.   When you feel anxious, do you ever lose your appetite?

2.   How do noise, a tight schedule, and crowds affect your appetite?

3.   Are teachers, parents, and school administrators the only individuals that may have concern and try to formulate solutions to problems that students with Asperger Syndrome experience in school?

Breaks

Although all students need breaks during the day, sometimes students who have Asperger Syndrome have difficulty with these unstructured periods. In grade school, the breaks usually occur one or two times during the school day when the students are encouraged to go outside and play ball games or use the playground. The playground times are troublesome for students with Asperger Syndrome because they are unstructured and often not very well supervised. Additionally, playground time usually requires social interaction with peers.

Usually, these playground periods include many students. Most of these students may be unfamiliar to the student with Asperger Syndrome. This student may feel awkward about joining in with games or conversations with peers. Sometimes, because only a few aides supervise the breaks, bullies may be able to corner the student with Asperger Syndrome. Although all students need breaks to reenergize, these breaks may cause distress for the student with Asperger Syndrome.

Breaks are necessary for these students, as these times are periods in which the pressure to perform academically is removed. They can provide a welcome break from the rigors of the school day. There are several ways that students can use these breaks fully, to allow the student with Asperger Syndrome time to refresh himself, and gather his energy for the remainder of the school day.

Elaine was an elementary-school teacher who was trying to find a way to make her student with Asperger Syndrome, Omar, more comfortable during breaks. Omar was socially awkward in group situations. He did not know how to approach a group to start or join a conversation. Omar did well academically at school, but during breaks he found himself isolated from his peers.

When Omar approached his peers, the students did not readily include him because he did not want to talk about the current topic of the conversation. Instead, he had his own agenda and talked on and on, not considering if the students were bored or not listening. This behavior isolated Omar from his peers, because the students would begin to walk away when they saw Omar approaching.

Omar also tended to touch the students when he was talking to them, and the students were very sensitive about being touched. Most students, no matter what their age, do not enjoy being touched by their fellow students. There is a comfort zone that people like to have, and Omar repeatedly did not recognize this "zone."

Elaine wanted Omar to develop some social skills so that he would enjoy breaks. Omar had begun to tell Elaine that he did not want to go outside, and that the students teased him. Elaine usually was on her own break at this time, so she did not observe the problem first-hand until Omar started complaining and the playground aides approached her. Although Elaine had to give up some of her own preparation time to deal with this issue, she felt that it was important to Omar's social development and his self-esteem to solve this problem. She decided that she would observe what was occurring in the playground so that she could better assess the problem.

Elaine decided that Omar needed to understand why the students were not readily accepting him into their conversation. She sat Omar down one day after lunch when the other students were out at break and told him the two reasons that she thought the other students were not including him in their conversation.

Elaine said very concisely to Omar, "The students have difficulty including you in the conversation because of two things. First, you do not like to talk about what they are interested in and, second, you touch them too much." Omar got a little upset because he felt that the students did not like him. However, Elaine assured him that if he could follow the two rules that she would tell him, conversations with the students would become much easier.

Elaine continued and said, "Omar, remember these two rules. The first rule is to listen to what the others are talking about and talk about the same subject. Rule two is not to touch any of the students." Elaine knew that when speaking to students with Asperger Syndrome she needed to be concrete and precise. She felt that these two rules would be easy for Omar to follow and remember during the break period. After their conversation, Elaine handed Omar a small card that had the two rules written on them. She also sent home a note for Omar's parents so that they would be able to reinforce the two rules at home.

Elaine discreetly talked to the students in the schoolyard group that Omar wanted to join. She told them that Omar wanted to join the group conversation and that he was using new strategies, so the students should give him another chance. The students included Omar in the conversation the next day. Omar remembered the rules and had an easier time joining the group discussion.

In time, Omar also learned that if he did not know anything about the topic, he could be quiet and listen, instead of changing the subject or saying something way off the topic. He also learned that people responded to him much better if he did not touch them or stand too close to them. The positive feedback of being included in the group made Omar want to learn more social rules. Elaine felt that she had succeeded in teaching Omar some appropriate social behaviors and boosting his self-esteem.

Ben had a different but similar problem to Omar. Ben was in Omar's grade and he had a teacher named Henry. Henry observed that Ben enjoyed physical activity at breaks and he wanted to join the other students when they were playing games.

However, Ben could not remember the rules of the games and got very flustered when there was a great deal of noise during the game playing. Ben has Asperger Syndrome. He has low muscle tone and poor coordination. These physical difficulties presented a challenge when Ben wanted to join in with physical games during breaks. Students with Asperger Syndrome can feel that playing games during breaks is even more challenging than playing games in a physical education class. The games during breaks are more unstructured and less supervised, and there is a higher level of peer interaction. Ben was so interested in playing these outside games that Henry decided he would try to find ways to help Ben interact appropriately with his peers as well as participate in the games.

Henry determined that Ben needed to know the rules of the games. Ben did not know how to play kickball or dodgeball, so he made many mistakes that made it difficult for him to interact with the other students. Henry made a card with the rules of kickball and another card with the rules of dodgeball, two of the most commonly played games at his school. He kept the instructions simple and clear. Henry kept a card in the classroom for Ben to look at prior to going out for break. He also gave Ben a card for him to take home and look at in the evenings. Henry also made another card that included daily, appropriate social skills that Ben would need to use whenever he had a break. Henry listed clear and simple rules such as: Keep your hands to yourself. Do not push. Do not yell. If you have a problem, go to the aide.

Henry reviewed this card with Ben daily until Ben had memorized the rules. Finally, during a break, Henry took Ben to the gym and actually practiced playing these outdoor games with him. Henry managed to get a couple of other students to play so that there were teams. In this way, Henry taught Ben how to learn the rules of the games and the skills needed for interacting on the playground during breaks.

After Ben felt confident that he could join the games and act appropriately on the playground, Henry observed Ben for several weeks. There were several occurrences where Ben got overwhelmed and Henry had to intervene. Henry gave suggestions to Ben based on his observation. Sometimes Ben was too rough with one of the other students and, at other times, Ben forgot the rules and acted inappropriately. By working slowly and consistently with Ben during breaks, Henry was able to involve Ben in the many games. Ben's self-confidence rose and he also participated more fully in physical education class.

Sometimes the student with Asperger Syndrome will choose to keep to himself during breaks. Students with Asperger Syndrome may use this time to decompress and think about their own interests. These students may also use breaks as a time to "get away" from the social pressures of school and may choose to be by themselves. This choice is perfectly appropriate for some students. However, the student with Asperger Syndrome should still be encouraged to go outside and walk around the playground to expend some energy. Sometimes, these students persever-ate; therefore, the student can use these breaks for a time to release pent-up energy.

Paul is a student with Asperger Syndrome. When he was in the third grade, he had an aide to help keep him focused during class. Paul often "flapped" his arms when he began to feel anxious or over-stimulated.

During breaks, Paul requested that his teacher permit him to go to the special education classroom instead of going outside. When Kelly, his teacher, asked why he wanted to stay inside, Paul indicated that he just did not like the outdoors. Kelly thought about his request, but she felt that Paul would benefit from fresh air, even if he did not interact with his peers at that time. Kelly decided that she needed to give Paul some ideas to use breaks fully so that Paul would benefit from the "down time." She suggested that if Paul feels anxious and he needs to "flap" he should walk around the perimeter of the schoolyard. This way he would exercise his body to reduce anxiety and possibly reduce the need to perseverate. She also told Paul that the walking would be a good way to think through some school issues that may be bothering him. Finally, she reminded Paul that walking around the schoolyard is a good way to "blend in" with the rest of the school students.

Kelly also suggested that if Paul needs an escape from his day, he could sit on a bench and read a magazine that he has brought from home. He could also read a library book, but Kelly emphasized that breaks should be "his time" and Paul should read or do something that he would find enjoyable. Kelly mentioned that Paul could also think about his favorite topics, such as video games, and make plans for his after-school activity. By doing this, Paul would remember that the school day does end, and he could focus on the enjoyment he gets when he is at home. Paul liked all the suggestions that Kelly gave him and agreed to try the outdoors instead of sitting in the special education classroom during his break.

Summary of strategies

1. Find out first-hand the problem the student has during breaks.

2. Give clear, concise rules regarding rules of conversation among peers.

3. Teach the student with Asperger Syndrome the rules about interacting with peers in a conversation (e.g. that he should stick to the topic that other students are discussing, that he should not touch other students).

4. Let the peers know that the student with Asperger Syndrome may need some help in the area of conversation skills.

5. Provide the student with Asperger Syndrome with rules listed on cards for the games that students play during breaks.

6. Provide the student with cards listing interaction rules while playing games.

7. Teach the student to play the games in a controlled setting to make sure he knows the rules and is comfortable playing the games.

8. Observe the playground interactions for several weeks and intervene if necessary until the student understands the rules.

9. Encourage outdoor activity that is not stressful for the student.

Points for reflection

1. Consider ways to encourage the student with Asperger Syndrome to try different environments that may be beneficial for him.

2. The student with Asperger Syndrome may feel isolated from his peers during breaks. What are some of the feelings that he may experience? Why is it important to have the student interact with peers, even if it is difficult at first?

Clubs

In many schools, clubs are offered to students before, during, or after school hours. Clubs provide students with a time to further academic knowledge or to have fun and socialize in a semi-structured setting. For a student with Asperger Syndrome, club periods can be taxing since socialization skills are usually required. If parents desire a student with Asperger Syndrome to become involved in a club period, teachers recommend that school personnel incorporate the club period into the school day since additional time added to the school day may be too burdensome for the student with Asperger Syndrome. Clubs provide an excellent way for the student to learn social skills in a smaller group without academic pressure. If the student wants to participate in a club, he should be encouraged to do so.

One way to get the student with Asperger Syndrome interested in a club is for the teacher who knows the student's interests to involve the student with planning the theme and activities of the club. The emphasis of the club should be fun and the teacher needs to be sure not to overwhelm the student.

Charlotte is a third-grade teacher who believed that she could convince Colin to be involved in a club. She had a good rapport with Colin and approached him about starting a computer club because he loved computers. Initially, Colin was enthusiastic about the club. Charlotte had put Colin in charge of making posters to advertise the club and to plan the activities of the club. Colin quickly lost interest in the club because the planning seemed too much like schoolwork for him.

Charlotte thought that the club would help Colin learn to interact with his peers and would be beneficial to his overall socialization at school, but realized that to make the club fun for Colin she would have to do the planning and preparation, and just allow him to work on his computer. She did all the preparatory work such as thinking of activities and getting classmates to join.

Charlotte observed the interactions that Colin had with the students during the club and she discreetly instructed both Colin and the others in socially appropriate behavior. Charlotte also assigned Colin to be the leader of the club and had him share his knowledge of computers. By showing the other members of the club that Colin was an "expert" in computers, she boosted Colin's self-confidence. She also helped the other students view Colin as having a special talent, which helped him in making friends with his classmates. Although the computer club was initially difficult for Charlotte to plan and execute, she felt that the result for Colin was better than she had expected.

Charlie, a middle-school teacher, works with Ioan, a student with Asperger Syndrome, in his Technology Education class. Charlie has a cousin with Asperger Syndrome and knows about some of the symptoms of Asperger Syndrome. Charlie decided that, since Ioan likes video games, he would start a video-game club during the weekly school club period. After receiving permission from his principal, Charlie selected one student to participate in his new club with Ioan. Ioan and the other student enjoyed playing video games for one month, and then Charlie introduced a new member to the club. At first, Ioan felt uncomfortable allowing the new member into the club since he was very fanatical about the video games. He did not think that anyone would understand how he felt about these games. Ioan discussed his feelings with his parents and Charlie. Both his parents and Charlie suggested that other students may have similar feelings about video games and that Ioan may want to listen to their feelings. Ioan talked to the new club members to find out how these students felt about these games. In time, he felt that he was part of a cohesive group.

Every month Charlie would add a new player to the club. The slow addition of group members assisted Ioan in making new acquaintances. The year culminated by having a video-game tournament. Ioan realized that others shared his passion for video games.

Summary of strategies

1. Club periods need to be incorporated into the school day schedule.

2. Club periods need to be a consistent part of the weekly routine at school.

3. Introduce new members to the group gradually.

4. Review Social Stories™ with the student.

5. Choose an area of student interest to help him feel comfortable with the club setting.

6. Incorporate social skills and appropriate social behaviors into the club setting.

7. Allow other students to see the student with Asperger Syndrome as an "expert" to help him gain self-confidence.

8. Make the club fun for the student with Asperger Syndrome, so he looks forward to attending.

Points for reflection

1. What is the desired outcome of the student participating in clubs?

2. How will you choose group members?

3. How could the club help a student with Asperger Syndrome to gain social skills?

End of the day

The end of the day usually presents a challenge for the student with Asperger Syndrome. The student, like most of the other students, is tired and fatigued from the long day at school. The end of the day is a period with two different tasks that could prove difficult for the student with Asperger Syndrome. First, the student needs to organize himself, his belongings and his books for the trip home. Second, he needs to transition to the home environment and after-school activities.

Since students with Asperger Syndrome usually have a hard time organizing under the best circumstances, the end of the day organizational requirements can be daunting for this student. Additionally, the end of the day is generally unsupervised and unstructured. Usually, the student ends the day in his homeroom and the students do not have specific tasks aside from the organizational aspects of this time. Therefore, the students usually interact or chat with each other.

These social activities also present a problem for the student with Asperger Syndrome, as he may lack the required social skills to engage in an appropriate conversation. Since the time is so unstructured and some students tend not know what to do with themselves, the student with Asperger Syndrome may feel anxious.

For students who ride school buses, this period is also when the students need to listen carefully as the teacher calls the bus numbers. Since the room is often noisy, and a student with Asperger Syndrome may have noise sensitivity, this student may have some legitimate worries about whether or not he will hear his bus number being called.

The homeroom teachers can use simple strategies to address these problems. Consider the following case of Roger, a seventh-grade student, and his teacher, Craig.

Craig noticed that although Roger was quiet at the end of day, he seemed extremely anxious. Craig taught Roger science and, although Roger was animated and appropriate in science class, he tended to be withdrawn during the last period of the day.

Craig observed Roger and noticed that he also quietly flapped to himself during that last period of the day. He did not organize his books and needed Craig to remind him to get his jacket on before racing out to the bus. Roger's mother also called the school frequently to try to get Roger's books because he neglected to bring home his homework. Additionally, Roger missed the bus frequently and his mother had to pick him up at school. After giving the matter some thought, Craig discovered certain ways in which he could make the transition at the end of the school day easier for Roger.

Craig gave Roger several "jobs" to do at the end of the school day. Roger had to make sure that he turned the computers off and that the erasers were put in the right spot. Craig wrote these two jobs on a small piece of paper that Roger kept in the front of his binder.

After Roger did these jobs, he needed to get his coat and bookbag and place them on his desk so he was ready to go home. Craig wrote these two tasks on a corner of the board and kept them there permanently to remind all students of their focus at the end of the day. Finally, Craig told Roger that after all the jobs had been finished and he was ready to leave, Roger could play on a computer. This idea worked for Roger because he loved playing games and making pictures on the computer. He had an incentive to do the jobs to be able to get computer time.

The computer that Roger used was in the corner of the room, away from many of the distractions of the class. Roger enjoyed the extra computer time. Craig assigned a student who rode the same bus with Roger to tell Roger when it was time to go. Since Roger was already prepared to leave, it did not take him long to gather his things and leave. He rarely missed the bus as he used the peer helper to guide him through the last hectic minutes of his day.

Summary of strategies

1. Identify the problems that the student is having at the end of the day to determine what help he needs.

2. Decrease the student's unstructured time by giving him jobs that he needs to do during the end of the day class period. List these jobs on the front of the student's binder so he will remember the jobs to be completed.

3. List on the board the organizational items that the student needs to do at the end of the day.

4. After the student is finished with his tasks, allow him some time to do a preferred interest activity (e.g. reading, computers).

5. Have a peer helper let the student know when it is time to leave the classroom for the bus, if this is a problem for the student.

Points for reflection

1. Remember that the end of the day is stressful for most students because they are tired from the long day. How do you feel at the end of a workday? What do you need to feel re-energized?

2. Focus on simple ways to help the student. At the end of the day, try not to place too many demands on the student. Again, consider your own feelings and energy level at the end of the day.

3. Can you think of another task that the student may enjoy at the end of the day, based on the student's needs and personality?

4. Is the noise level in your classroom very high at the end of day? Consider ways that you could reduce the overall noise level, which may benefit all the students.

5. Think of ways you relax prior to leaving the classroom and consider these ideas as possibilities for all the students.

Special theme, track and field days

In the elementary grades, the routine of the normal school day is sometimes broken up by special theme days, such as the birthday of a prominent figure. On these days, the teachers often request that the students wear something different. The students may attend an assembly about the particular day. Schools also have some week-long activities, when on each day of the week the students need to wear something different, such as funny slippers or hats, to school.

While most students find these days a welcome break from the daily routine, students with Asperger Syndrome may find the days unpredictable and scary. Especially in the younger grades, when the student is not used to these types of days, the disruption in routine may cause uncertainty and stress. Teachers who have students with Asperger Syndrome in their classroom need to give these students plenty of warning about what will happen on these days.

The teachers also need to be aware that although the student with Asperger Syndrome seems to be handling the disruption in routine admirably, the student may have a tantrum or meltdown later in the day, many hours from the time of the special event. During the special days, the teacher should be extremely aware of any worry or anxiety that the student shows.

Another event, which occurs each year and can be difficult for the student with Asperger Syndrome, is track and field day. Track and field day includes a good deal of physical activity with the students competing in sports and other activities. The students do very little academic work on this day. Although the day may be fun for many students, often the student with Asperger Syndrome sees track and field day as a horrible day that he may dread for months. Sometimes, the only solution is to have the student kept at home for track and field day. However, the teachers may make some accommodations regarding track and field day as is shown in the following story.

Gregory was a student in third grade and has Asperger Syndrome. He was rather clumsy and did not like athletics. He was also very sensitive to temperature and he could not tolerate prolonged standing or playing in the sun. Gregory preferred to stay indoors much of the time. Gregory was very nervous about track and field day. He told his mom that he did not want to go to school on that day. His mother felt that Gregory should attempt to attend track and field day. She called Barry, Gregory's teacher, to let him know that she was planning to send Gregory to school on track and field day. However, she asked that Barry make some accommodations for Gregory.

Barry was glad that Gregory's mother had decided to send him to school for track and field day. The other students regarded Gregory as somewhat different, and Barry did not want Gregory to stand out even more. Barry decided he would accommodate as much as possible for Gregory during track and field day, so that Gregory would have a positive experience and would want to participate in later years.

About a week before track and field day, Barry reminded his students that track and field day was quickly approaching. He briefly described the activities. Barry then handed a schedule out for all the students so they could get used to what would happen during the day. Gregory began to clap his hands together, which meant that he was becoming agitated. Barry told the rest of the class to start an assignment and then quietly called Gregory to his desk.

When asked, Gregory told Barry that he was very scared about track and field day because he thought he would not be able to participate in any of the activities and that everyone would tease him. For a student without a disorder, Barry would have given the usual reply: that the student would be okay, that the day would be fun, and that he just needs to try his best. However, Barry knew that track and field day would be a challenge for Gregory. Barry therefore reassured Gregory that he understood the reasons that Gregory was afraid and that he would work on ways that he could make the day better for Gregory. He did not tell Gregory exactly what he was going to do, but he felt sure that he could do something to help him participate in track and field day.

Barry checked the weather for the day that track and field day was scheduled and the weather forecast was to be hot and humid. Barry sent a note home with Gregory specifically requesting that Gregory bring in enough water to get him through the day in the heat. He also requested that Gregory bring in a small battery-powered fan, and wear a hat to keep the sunrays off his face. Barry surveyed the track and field day layout and found a spot that was near the activities, but that was in a shaded area.

Gregory was not very good at athletics, but he happened to be an excellent "cup stacker." Since track and field day teaches students about competition and fair play, Barry approached the physical education teacher to request that "cup stacking" be included as a new event. "Cup stacking" is a game that encourages team cooperation. It is a good game to reinforce socialization skills. The physical education teachers agreed to add this as an event. Gregory was ecstatic that he would get to participate in a sport that he was good at and enjoyed. Since the students were only required to be in one event, Gregory relaxed. He actually began to look forward to track and field day, knowing that his teacher had found ways to make track and field day fun for him.

Summary of strategies

1.   For special days, tell the students what will occur on those days about a week in advance, so the student with Asperger Syndrome can prepare himself for the upcoming change in routine.

2.   Provide a schedule for the special theme day several days before the actual event.

3.   For track and field day, determine the special needs and sensitivities of the student with Asperger Syndrome. Make accommodations for the student based on this information.

4.   If the student has difficulty with athletics, find some other sport that he can participate in and incorporate that sport into the track and field day events.

Points for reflection

1.   Did you enjoy track and field day when you were in grade school? Do you think there could be a different type of track and field day for students who are not naturally athletic?

2.   How do you feel about a teacher making accommodations for a student who does not have obvious physical problems for track and field day type activities?

CHAPTER 5

Social and Emotional Concerns

A teacher who has a student with Asperger Syndrome in her classroom needs to know more about that student than the "typical" student in her classroom. The teacher will need to have knowledge of this student's personality, strengths, and weaknesses so the teacher can help him become a successful part of the school community.

The teacher's additional knowledge about the student is necessary because the teacher may notice different social and emotional concerns arise when a student has Asperger Syndrome. When an incident occurs that requires discipline, school personnel need to obtain more information to assess the situation. Communicating with parents is imperative to help school staff understand how the student with Asperger Syndrome feels.

Discipline

Disciplining a student with Asperger Syndrome can be a complex process. The person who feels that there is a need for discipline should be sure that the behavior was caused by the student's desire to misbehave, as opposed to the symptoms of Asperger Syndrome. Some students with Asperger Syndrome are disruptive on purpose. For others, the disruption of making noises in class or perseverating is an expression of the student's anxiety due to some environmental or other stress. Therefore, before proceeding to discipline a student with Asperger Syndrome, someone who knows the student well must evaluate the entire scenario.

If the student did misbehave, then the teacher or principal may need to give a consequence for the behavior. The most effective consequence will teach the student with Asperger Syndrome about dealing with a particular stress or choosing a better behavior next time. Additionally, if the incident involved another student, the teacher can use the consequence of the incident to teach the student with Asperger Syndrome about appropriate peer relationships. If the teacher uses an incident to teach the student a better behavior and some social skills, the "bad behavior incident" can become an excellent way for the student with Asperger Syndrome to learn appropriate skills.

The teacher needs to be careful that she does not make the student feel shame or guilt for his behavior. Students with Asperger Syndrome often feel embarrassment about their odd behaviors. The teacher will not want to exacerbate this feeling in the student. After the entire discipline process is complete, the student should feel that he learned something and that he has the skills to deal with a similar situation in a different way. This approach to discipline may seem like it is too "soft" on the student. However, teachers and school staff must remember that students with Asperger Syndrome have a disability that can cause non-typical behaviors.

Donald has Asperger Syndrome. He showed classic symptoms of the disorder, including some lack of impulse control. Additionally, Donald was socially awkward, and did not know how to read the emotions of other students very well. As an eighth-grade student, Donald was well behaved, but school staff sent Donald to the principal's office occasionally for disciplinary issues. The typical situation that led to Donald's misbehavior occurred when the students had unstructured time at the end of class periods or at the end of the day. Often, these times were noisy and had minimal teacher supervision.

On one of these days, Donald's classmates started to tease him about liking a fellow classmate, Jackie. Jackie had given Donald attention previously, but he was clearly not interested in pursuing a friendship with her. Donald understandably became upset when the three students said that Jackie and Donald should get married, and that they should kiss each other. Donald was unsure what to do or say. Consequently, he became very anxious and perseverated by flapping his arms.

The noise level in the room increased and the three students said something to Donald again. At that point, Donald walked over to one of the students and bit him on the neck. He also grabbed one of the other students and tried to strangle him. Donald was bigger than both of these students so the students called for help. The teacher saw what was going on and told Donald to leave the room and wait in the hallway. She then sent Donald to the principal's office.

The principal, Risa, was familiar with Donald because she had seen him on several other occasions. Risa had a background in special education and was familiar with the symptoms and behaviors of students with Asperger Syndrome. Risa had an idea of what happened, because she knew that Donald was not a "bad" kid. However, she was bound by the rules of the school to do something about Donald's behavior. Risa talked to the students and the teacher of the class to determine what had happened. She decided that it was important that Donald understand that he needs to keep his hands off the students, no matter how he feels.

Risa thought this was an important concept for Donald to learn because, as he got older, touching people inappropriately could result in being ostracized by others and could possibly lead to criminal charges being filed against him. Risa decided that she needed to do something to make Donald realize that this behavior was not acceptable, no matter what the reason.

Risa determined several consequences for Donald's action. She called Donald into her office and made sure that Donald knew what it was he did that was inappropriate. Risa emphasized that Donald had grabbed the students and that grabbing, touching, and biting others is not acceptable in school. She told Donald that a rule that he needs to memorize is that he is not to touch anyone at school.

Donald was sad when he heard the rule, because he said he felt he should be able to do high-fives. Risa emphasized that Donald needed to show her and others that he could memorize and learn the "no touching" rule before she could make exceptions. Donald reluctantly agreed that he needed to learn to remember not to touch others at school and that he would try to remember the rule.

Risa chose this method of relating to Donald because she knew that students with Asperger Syndrome often think in concrete terms. Risa thought that Donald would remember a one-sentence rule. Risa also thought she could teach Donald a social skill regarding how to apologize to someone who has been hurt. Risa had Donald write an apology letter to the boys that he had bothered. Donald was willing to do this because he had thought of those boys as friends of his and he wanted to continue the friendship.

Risa told Donald that it was good to write an apology letter because then Donald would not have to feel uncomfortable about his past behavior when he sees the boys in class again. She told Donald that the apology letter is an end to the incident and that Donald did not need to discuss the incident with anyone again.

Finally, Risa told Donald that he would need to stay after school in detention for one day because he needed to have a negative consequence for his behavior. This way Donald would remember that his behavior was inappropriate. Donald understood the reason for the detention. Risa also chose to give Donald the detention because she did not want him to feel that he was different from other students who acted inappropriately.

Donald left Risa's office feeling relieved that the incident was over and that he received his consequence. Now he could stop thinking about what he did. The reason why these consequences worked for Donald was that Risa gave extra thought to the cause of the behavior and the way that she explained to Donald what he had done wrong. She did not make him feel bad about himself. Instead, she gave him a rule to think about if the situation should arise again.

As a follow-up to this incident, Risa had the teacher schedule a session on bullying for the entire class. Risa also looked into scheduling an assembly for the entire school about acting appropriately with their peers.

Risa made sure that she also made a phone call to Donald's parents, to let them know what had happened and how she handled the situation. She welcomed input from the parents about Donald's behavior.

Summary of strategies

1. Get to know the symptoms of Asperger Syndrome so that you can determine what behaviors arise from the disorder and what actions you can consider to be intentional misbehaviors.

2. Make sure to approach the student with Asperger Syndrome in a gentle, understanding way when correcting his behaviors.

3. Have the student take responsibility for his actions and explain the consequences of his behaviors.

4. Give the student a concrete rule to follow that will help him avoid the poor behavior choice.

5. Have the student learn about the other person's feelings by including a letter of apology as part of the consequence, if appropriate.

6. Give the student an appropriate consequence that would be similar to other students' consequences. This way he may feel that he is not so different from other students.

7. Communicate the incident and consequence to the student's parents and listen to their input.

8. Be creative in assigning disciplinary action.

Points for reflection

1. Given the hectic pace of the school, students who disrupt the flow are often determined to be discipline problems. Do you feel you can slow down enough to assess the poor behavior of a student with Asperger Syndrome? What could you do to remind yourself to deal with this student gently?

2. Have you ever thought about discipline as a way to teach positive social skills? Imagine how you would change your current discipline procedure when dealing with a student with Asperger Syndrome.

3. Do you feel that the parents help or hinder the discipline of a student with Asperger Syndrome?

Communicating with parents

Parents can be an important resource for teachers when they have a student with Asperger Syndrome in their classroom. The parents of the student with Asperger Syndrome need to be involved, supportive, and helpful to the teacher for the teacher to be able to use the parents' knowledge of the child effectively. If the teacher senses that the parents of the student with Asperger Syndrome are not responsive to her communications, it is better if the teacher accommodates the student without parental involvement. Although this is more difficult for the teacher, negative parents can adversely affect the relationship between the teacher and the student.

This section focuses on the ways that parents can be useful to teachers when accommodating for the student with Asperger Syndrome. The section also discusses the different ways for teachers to communicate with the parents. The teacher will note that even parents of students without difficulties may appreciate some of the methods described below.

Teachers of students without difficulties may or may not know the parents of each of their students very well. Often, a teacher may feel that it is never necessary to contact some parents. If there is a slight problem, a teacher's brief phone call to the parents can usually resolve the issue. However, the relationship that a teacher has with the parents of students with Asperger Syndrome is drastically different. If the student is to be successful at school, he needs much more support from both his parents and the teacher. Often, the student will also need either a classroom aide or personal aide to guide him through his day. Constant communication between all of the student's support persons is essential for any plan to work effectively.

Prior to the beginning of the school year, the primary teacher who will be in charge of the student should call the parents to arrange a time for a meeting. In elementary school, the primary support for the student with Asperger Syndrome will be the teacher. In higher-grade levels, the student may have one teacher assigned as the lead teacher or main point of contact. The lead teacher is the teacher who the parents will communicate with directly and most often.

After the initial phone call and meeting, the teacher needs to establish a consistent way of contacting the parent. Often, the student with Asperger Syndrome is not a reliable messenger. For example, due to organizational issues, the student may misplace materials (e.g. notes home). Communication with parents may include contact by telephone, email, or daily written communication (placed by the teacher in the student's bookbag or backpack). The teacher and parents may benefit by establishing a "best time to call" procedure. At the beginning of the school year, the parent can provide important information to the teacher as she is preparing for the school year.

It is important that the teacher obtain as much information as she can about the student with Asperger Syndrome from the parents, because the teacher will not really know the student until several months into the school year. The parents can inform the teacher about the student's sensitivities and other problem areas. More specifically, the parents can provide valuable information about the following: the student's difficulties, temperament, family life, reactions to stress, and discipline at home. The parents can also let the teacher know the student's reaction to new strategies and give the teacher feedback on the student's anxiety level.

Since the parents have long-term knowledge of the student, they can also provide insight into what has worked and not worked in the past. The parents can also communicate to the teacher the student's point of view about incidents that may have occurred at school. The student may be too shy or overwhelmed to relate the experience directly to the school personnel. Hearing the student's side of the story may shed light on things that the teacher needs to change in the student's school day. The student's version of an incident can help the teacher to determine the most appropriate discipline for the situation.

Sherry is the case manager for Howard, a student in eighth grade who has Asperger Syndrome. Sherry had found Howard's mother to be an invaluable source of information and feedback for helping Howard to be successful at school. Sherry has access to email and frequently emails Howard's mother about his assignments. Sherry also asks questions about Howard's stress level. Usually, Howard's mother can provide information that helps Sherry in making decisions. Sherry remembers the day when Howard was very agitated in the morning. He was upset and unable to concentrate. Sherry tried her usual strategies to calm Howard. She let him have "flap time," and permitted him to eat lunch in her classroom where it was quiet and Howard could use the computer. Howard was still upset but he did not tell Sherry why. Howard kept repeating, "Franklin is an idiot, an idiot."

After lunch, Sherry decided to email Howard's mother to see what was happening in Howard's life to make him upset. Howard's mother explained that one of the neighborhood children named Franklin had teased Howard last evening and would not let him participate in the neighborhood game of "Capture the Flag." Normally, Howard would not have been interested in playing, but on this particular night he was, and Franklin said Howard could not play because he was slow and he flapped. Howard's mother reported that although she talked to Howard about the situation, Howard was still upset and that was why he was acting in an agitated manner.

Since she was given this information, Sherry was able to coax Howard to tell his story to the guidance counselor and ask for her advice. Sherry made an appointment with the counselor for Howard at the end of the day. After the meeting, Howard returned to Sherry's class and thanked her for making the suggestion. Without the input of Howard's mother, the situation would not have been resolved as quickly or easily. Parental involvement is one key for success for the students with Asperger Syndrome.

Summary of strategies

1.   Determine whether the parents of the student with Asperger Syndrome will be helpful communicators.

2.   Find a reliable, easy way to communicate with the parents of the student with Asperger Syndrome.

3.   Try to develop a rapport with the parents of the student with Asperger Syndrome by keeping them updated on schedule changes and informed about the student's progress, both academically and socially.

4. Do not hesitate to contact the parents to get information about the student if the student seems uncharacteristically withdrawn, upset, or out of sorts.

Points for reflection

1. Do you avoid parental contact as a general practice?

2. Does it seem that parental contact should not be part of your job as a teacher? How can you look at the parental contact in a more positive way?

3. Do you feel that having parents involved with a student would be an intrusion or a help?

Preventing bullying and educating students about Asperger Syndrome

Students with Asperger Syndrome often stand out in the class and, because of their differences, the students are often the target of bullying and teasing. Students with Asperger Syndrome are often misunderstood. For example, inappropriate behaviors have led to these students being regarded as willfully disruptive by their teachers and as obnoxious by their peers. While it is true that any student with or without Asperger Syndrome has the capacity to have discipline problems, more often than not poor social and school behaviors are a result of the disorder.

Like teachers, other students need to understand a little about why students with Asperger Syndrome have such "quirky" behaviors. A little understanding and knowledge can go a long way to show other students how to assist easily, rather than ignore or taunt a student with Asperger Syndrome.

Judy is a middle-school social studies teacher. She was distraught when she saw how some students were treating Alison, a student with Asperger Syndrome. Students would laugh at Alison and bait her to say silly things. Alison had no idea why her classmates were being cruel to her and why they did not like her. She thought of herself as a kind, generous person. Alison has a couple of friends, but she does not know how to deal with taunting.

Alison's parents did not know how to help the situation. Judy talked to the school psychologist about this situation because she was concerned about Alison's mental health. The school psychologist and Judy devised a plan to help Alison. Part of the plan involved Judy teaching Alison social skills. A larger part of the plan used the school staff to implement procedures to stop students from being unkind to Alison.

Judy talked with Alison's parents about teaching her students about Asperger Syndrome. They agreed that Alison would not be present in the room when the lessons took place as, although Judy would not divulge confidential information about Alison, the discussion about the details of Asperger Syndrome in the presence of Alison's peers may be difficult for Alison to hear. Later, however, Alison would be included in the discussion.

Judy and the school psychologist presented a mini-lesson regarding Asperger Syndrome, including the reasons that students with this disorder may have difficulty with some social situations. The school psychologist gave suggestions to the students regarding how to help a classmate with Asperger Syndrome.

The school psychologist prepared Alison before the second session, where she would be present. Alison explained to her classmates the times when she felt uncomfortable in school and how she felt when the students taunted her. She also talked about how she would like her classmates to treat her and how her classmates could help to make her school day more bearable.

It is important to point out that Judy and the school psychologist discussed the situation with the school principal. While peer understanding of Asperger Syndrome is important, it is also necessary for all students to know the consequences for bullying. All of Alison's teachers were informed about the lessons and they were all asked to monitor the situation. In addition, the staff spoke as a unified voice in letting students know that they would not tolerate any bullying.

The majority of students stopped bullying Alison. One student teased Alison so the principal disciplined the student and his parents were informed. Word got around among the students that the staff and administration were serious about bullying.

A few students volunteered to help Alison carry her books (she has trouble with carrying around her backpack), and they offered to help her to navigate the hallways.

Summary of strategies

1. Directly teach students about Asperger Syndrome.

2. Communicate consequences for bullying to students.

3. Encourage students to help each other with any difficulty they may be having in school. Build a culture of cooperation and respect for one another.

Points for reflection

1. How are individuals viewed when they appear to be different from the normal group?

2. Have you ever been teased? How did it feel?

3. Did you receive help in school from your peers?

4. How can you teach students to assist their peers in school?

Social skills lessons

Students with Asperger Syndrome often do not understand the unwritten rules of social relationships. Teachers must teach directly to the student with Asperger Syndrome the lessons that most individuals take for granted and learn indirectly. For example, body language speaks volumes about a person. Most people understand that when speaking with a classmate, individuals keep their hands to themselves, keep a small distance, and do not speak too loudly. Students with Asperger Syndrome do not necessarily understand this concept and need a teacher to explain it to them.

Students with Asperger Syndrome may not modulate their tone of voice well, may stand too close to another person in conversation, and may touch another person at inappropriate times. Additionally, students with Asperger Syndrome sometimes have difficulty making and keeping friends. Often, these students do not understand how to make effective small talk. For most individuals conversations are two-sided. Individuals ask each other questions and respond to each other. Students with Asperger Syndrome often have certain preoccupations or obsessions with objects or activities. The students' conversations focus around their own interests. It is difficult to talk with an individual when he only talks about himself.

Social skills lessons can be as little as ten minutes long (mini-lessons) or as long as is practical. The purpose of social skills lessons is to teach directly to students with Asperger Syndrome what most other students learn without direct instruction. Teachers, counselors, or other staff members can provide these lessons.

Suzanne is a high-school counselor. Her job includes meeting with groups of students and discussing coping and anger management skills, and achieving success in school. Suzanne initiated a group to help students who seemed to have difficulty socially interacting with their peers. Many students, not just those with Asperger Syndrome, experience such difficulties.

Suzanne invited eight students together for an ongoing group. Two of the students have Asperger Syndrome. The focus of the group, which meets once every two weeks, is to help students learn and practice good social skills. The skills include appropriate greetings, making "small talk," and making and keeping friends. Suzanne gave homework assignments such as to practice saying "Hello" and "Goodbye" while smiling.

After a few weeks of the group, Suzanne's students with and without Asperger Syndrome reported to be more comfortable with their peers. Suzanne noticed her students talked more with others and seemed to have a happier demeanor. It is not surprising that students can benefit from a social skills lesson. In fact, there are a great many books written about etiquette for adults.

Teachers instruct their students about appropriate behaviors. Direct instructions from teachers to all students about maintaining relationships is appropriate and effective. Even without school counseling groups, teachers are in a good position to assist students with Asperger Syndrome by providing support and advice on an ongoing basis or as needed for these students.

Summary of strategies

1. Teach conversation skills to students with Asperger Syndrome directly.

2. Teach students with Asperger Syndrome about proper body language, voice modulation, and appropriate proximity to others during conversations.

3. Involve students with and without Asperger Syndrome in social skills lessons.

4. Lesson can be short, on an ongoing basis, or as needed.

5. Teachers, counselors, and other staff can teach social skills to students with Asperger Syndrome.

Points for reflection

1. Do teachers instruct all students in appropriate social skills?

2. Is it the responsibility of school staff to help students with Asperger Syndrome to develop appropriate peer relationships?

3. Do school staff have the time to be helping students with Asperger Syndrome in this regard?

Stress reduction

Students with Asperger Syndrome usually experience a high degree of anxiety in school. Sometimes these students do not have the ability to verbalize their concerns. Instead, they may deal with feelings of anxiety by flapping, having meltdowns, or even wetting their pants. Sometimes students with Asperger Syndrome will call out in class and leave their seats. Students can benefit from learning school expectations and procedures as this knowledge can help lessen their worries about current and future school experiences.

Individuals of all ages use stress reduction activities to help them cope with everyday life. Teachers have used opportunities during the school day to give students with Asperger Syndrome some time to relax and reflect.

Julian is a middle-school mathematics teacher who has taken a particular liking to Terry, a student with Asperger Syndrome. Terry's mathematics class is in the middle of the day, right after his lunch period. Terry often feels stressed during lunch because of the large numbers of people, the loud noises, and commotion. The students have a ten-minute period after lunch before class starts in which the students can work on homework and get individual support from their teacher. Julian, being a practitioner of yoga, believes that stress reduction has a place in school for all students, and in particular for Terry.

Julian decided to give Terry a stress reduction activity each day following lunch. First, he taught Terry how to make healthy deep breaths. He also gave Terry a stress ball to use and gave him an opportunity to take a walk with a peer. Julian experimented with ways of relaxation that would work specifically for Terry. Julian decided to let Terry go to the library, where it is always quiet, to read some favorite reading material.

During this time, Terry breathes slowly and deliberately and simply enjoys being in a quiet area, with no distractions. There are a couple of beanbag chairs in the library and Terry feels comfortable in these chairs. After lunch each day, Terry has a written pass allowing him and a peer to go to the library. Terry has a friend in class that likes to help him. This simple stress reduction activity helps Terry regain focus so he can concentrate on academic tasks after lunch. Julian monitors this activity to make sure that it continues to work. He knows that Terry's needs may change over time; however, Terry will probably always need stress reduction.

Summary of strategies

1. Experiment with ways of helping students with Asperger Syndrome to relax in school.

2. Provide special accommodations in school where the student can be engaged in some sort of stress reduction activity.

3.   Typical stress reduction techniques may not work in school for students with Asperger Syndrome. For example, deep breathing and meditation activities, while they may work for many individuals, may not be a preferred activity for students with Asperger Syndrome.

4.   Distractions such as reading a favorite magazine and being away from groups of people may be effective ways of reducing stress.

5.   Monitor stress reduction activities for effectiveness over time. It may be helpful to modify or change these activities after a period to keep the student's interest.

Points for reflection

1.   What do you do to reduce stress?

2.   Can schools be stressful places for adults and students and, if so, why?

3.   Do the same stress reduction techniques work for everyone?

4.   Who needs to learn stress reduction techniques other than students with Asperger Syndrome?

Conclusion

Students with Asperger Syndrome pose a challenge for educators. With some simple, creative, and fun accommodations, these students can achieve success in school. Every teacher with whom we have worked who has taught a student with Asperger Syndrome has positive comments regarding his or her experiences. Many times, teachers report that they grew professionally and personally from learning about and helping students with this disorder. It is our belief that students with Asperger Syndrome are a gift to us as parents and educators. These students make educators reflect on their practices for all students. These students also help us develop compassion for individuals with differences who require special assistance. Finally, it is the responsibility of school personnel and parents to help to prepare students with Asperger Syndrome to be productive members of society.

Daily Homework Checklist

Goal: I plan to complete the following homework during _____ at school.

☐ Reading

☐ Math

☐ English

☐ Science

☐ Social Studies

☐ Other (Computer, Art, P.E.)

To do – homework I need to complete at home:

☐ Reading

☐ Math

☐ English

☐ Science

☐ Social Studies

☐ Other (Computer, Art, P.E.)

One positive thing I did today:

_____

_____

Parent signature: _____

✓

How to Help Your Classmate – Peer Helper Handout

My classmate's name: _____

My name: _____

What is Asperger Syndrome?

Asperger Syndrome is a problem that affects a person's sensory system. The sensory system controls how people see, smell, touch, taste, and hear. Sometimes a person with Asperger Syndrome has trouble with noise, bright lights, eating spicy foods, or with crowds. Additionally, some people with this condition have trouble when there are many changes.

My classmate's favorite things to do:

_____

Things my classmate really dislikes doing:

_____

Things that give my classmate trouble:

_____

My classmate's favorite foods:

_____

What my classmate needs help with:

_____

What my classmate and I like to do together:

_____

Student Information Form

Student name: _____

Date of birth: _____

Date of report: _____

Grade: _____

Family: _____

School personnel: _____

Bus transportation: _____

    Seating _____

Hallways: _____

    Navigating (with/without assistance) _____

    Accommodations _____

Homeroom: _____

    Noise level _____

    Routine _____

Class accommodations: _____

    Language Arts _____

    Mathematics _____

    Social Studies _____

    Science _____

    Electives _____

School activities accommodations: _____

    Assemblies _____

    School ceremonies _____

Breaks accommodations: _____

Sensitivities – taste, touch, smell, hearing, seeing: _____

Wait box items: _____

Visual or text schedule: _____

Hobbies/interests: _____

References

D.A.R.E. America (1996) *Drug Abuse Resistance Education (D.A.R.E.) Program.* Inglewood, CA: D.A.R.E. America. Available online: www.dare.com.

Discovery Communications, Inc. (2004) *City Life in Europe.* VHS Video. Silver Spring, MD: Discovery Communications, Inc.

Gray, C. (2000) *The New Social Stories Book* (2nd ed.). Arlington, TX: Future Horizons.

Lewandowski, A. (2000) *Orange World.* Software. Available online: http://igre.emich.edu/visit/Resource/guide/adding_data.htm.

Pyle, H., Hanft, J.E., and Pablo Marcus Studio (Corporate Author) (2002) *King Arthur and the Knights of the Round Table* (Great Illustrated Classics). Edina, MN: Abdo Publishing Company.

Shelton, R.L. (May 2001) *Statement of L. Robert Shelton Executive Director National Highway Traffic Safety Administration before the Subcommittee on Highways and Transit Committee on Transportation and Infrastructure U.S. House of Representatives.* Washington, DC: NHTSA. Available online: www.house.gov/transportation/highway/05-09-01/shelton.html.

Walker, L. (2001) The Crazy Critters. Melbourne: Pearson Longman. Available online: www.scriptsforschools.com/89.html.

Index